THE

CHRISTIAN WORLD UNMASKED.

BY

JOHN BERRIDGE, A.M.

VICAR OF EVERTON, BEDFORDSHIRE; FELLOW OF CLARE-HALL, CAMBRIDGE;
AND CHAPLAIN TO THE RIGHT HONORABLE THE
EARL OF BUCHAN.

WITH

LIFE OF THE AUTHOR,

BY THE

REV. THOMAS GUTHRIE, D.D.

MINISTER OF FREE ST. JOHN'S, EDINBURGH.

BOSTON:
GOULD AND LINCOLN,
59 WASHINGTON STREET.
1854.

Geo. C. Rand, Printer, 3 Cornhill, Boston.

INTRODUCTORY NOTE

TO THE

AMERICAN EDITION.

THIS work is republished from a recent Edinburgh edition. Some words and phrases, on account of their excessive quaintness or lack of dignity, have been expunged; and a few paragraphs containing irrelevant matter have been omitted.

It will be observed that many passages of Scripture are not quoted *verbatim;* but, as the words added or substituted are generally intended to be paraphrastic or expository, it has been thought best to leave them unaltered.

The author handles the word of God, not deceitfully, but skilfully, giving the sense of the sacred text with peculiar clearness and force. In a treatise less colloquial in style, his method of citation might be objectionable; but here it will be admired as an excellence. This facility in the use of Scripture is said to have given a special charm to his preaching.

To the Memoir furnished by Dr. Guthrie, is appended a striking notice of Berridge as a man and a preacher, from an article in the North British Review, giving an eloquent account of the men to whom the cause of evangelical religion in England was principally indebted, in the middle of the last century.

MEMOIR.

John Berridge, the author of this book, was, along with some others of his day, the salt of the Church of England, and an instrument in God's hand of working revivals of religion within her pale worthy of record with those that his compeers Whitefield and Wesley wrought without her. He was born in 1716, but not born again till he had entered the ministry. His studies were carried on at Cambridge, where he gave early proof of his native energy, and that what he did, as was said by an old woman of Dr. Chalmers, he did with all his heart. At that seat of learning, where he gained the honors and emoluments of a Fellowship, he passed for many years fifteen hours a day in hard study, ranging over all the fields of knowledge, and strengthening by such vigorous exercise faculties of no ordinary power. Clare College at length presented him to the charge of Everton in Bedfordshire, where he labored as few men have done, till his death, in 1793. In a short but most graphic sketch of our author, Dr. Hamilton, of London, thus relates the very quiet but remarkable way in which the Holy Spirit brought him to a saving knowledge of the truth :—"His success was small—so small that he began to suspect his mode was wrong. After prayer for light, it was one day borne in upon his mind—'Cease from thine own works, only believe ;' and, consulting his concordance, he was surprised to see how many columns were required for the words *Faith* and *Believe*. Through this quaint inlet he found his way into the knowledge of the Gospel, and the consequent love of the Saviour; and though hampered with academic standing, and past the prime of life, he did not hesitate for a moment to reverse his former preaching, and the efficiency of the cross was soon seen in his altered parish."

Nor were his labors confined to his parish now. He was not content with his own *preserve*. Not the man to stand by and see others beyond the parochial boundary perishing for lack of knowledge, he flung himself, heart and soul, into the very thick of the movement then being made by Lady Huntingdon, Venn, Grimshawe, Wesley, Whitefield, and others, to awaken England from its sleep of death ; and never but on one occasion did he allow consequences, personal, pecuniary, or ecclesiastical, to turn him a hairbreadth from the path of duty. We record it as an example of how God may ordain strength out of the mouths of babes and sucklings, and by the weak things of the church confound the strong :—" One day, during the period of his itinerancy, he had occasion to pass through a town where he had often met the scoffs and taunts of the ungodly ; but instead of riding through the main street, he turned through a bye-way to avoid the profane people who were in the streets. Here he was met by a pig-driver, who immediately addressed him, and said — 'You cowardly John Berridge, you are ashamed of your Master, and therefore you skulk along here to avoid the cross.' This incident, he said, was of incalculable benefit to him ; it spoke with effect to his heart, and he became more and more determined not to be moved in bold confession of Christ." That solitary occasion which found Berridge skulking down a bye lane to escape the insolence of the mob, but stands as a foil to the bravery with which he faced his bishop, armed with all the powers of the church to crush him. Fortunately Berridge has left this scene painted by his own hand :— " Soon after I began to preach the Gospel at Everton — says Mr. Berridge — the churches in the neighborhood were deserted, and mine so overcrowded, that the 'squire, who 'did not like strangers,' he said, 'and hated to be incommoded,' joined with the offended parsons, and soon after, a complaint having been made against me, I was summoned before the bishop. 'Well, Berridge, —said his lordship,—did I institute you to Eaton or Potton? Why do you go preaching out of your own parish?' 'My lord—said I,—I make no claim to the livings of those parishes. 'Tis true I was once at Eaton, and, finding a few poor people assembled, I admonished them to repent of their sins, and to believe in the Lord Jesus Christ for the salvation of their souls. At that very moment, my lord, there were five or six clergymen out of their own parishes, and enjoying themselves on the Eaton bowling-green.' 'I tell you—retorted his lordship,—that if you continue preaching where you have no right, you will very likely be sent to Huntingdon goal.' 'I have no more regard, my lord, for a goal than other folks—rejoined I,—but I had rather go *there* with a good conscience, than be at liberty without one.' His lordship looked very hard at me. 'Poor fellow!—said he,—you are beside yourself, and in a few months you will either be better or worse.' 'Then, my lord—said I,—you may make yourself quite happy in this business; for if I should be better, you suppose I shall desist of my own accord; and if worse, you need not send me to Huntingdon goal, for I shall be better accommodated in Bedlam.' His lordship then pathetically entreated me, as one who had been and wished to continue my friend, not to embitter the remaining portion of his days by any squabbles with my brother clergymen, but to go home to my parish, and so long as I kept within it I should be at liberty to do what I liked there. 'As to your conscience—said his lordship,—you know that preaching out of your parish is contrary to the canons of the Church.' 'There is one canon, my lord—said I,—which I dare not disobey, and that says, '*Go preach the Gospel to* EVERY CREATURE.'" It is worthy of notice that God raised up friends in unexpected quarters to shield this faithful servant. The great Lord Chatham came from the helm of the nation to stand between him and ruin; while the Lord Chancellor of England also was moved by Lady Huntingdon to leave the Woolsack and come to the rescue of the Vicar of Everton. In allusion to that circumstance, Grimshawe thus pithily and pathetically writes:—"May the Lord eternally bless that dear, good, honorable Lady Huntingdon, who would defend a persecuted minister of Christ to the last gown on her back, and the last shilling in her pocket."

For the trials and opposition which Berridge had to meet from many quarters, he had an ample recompense in the extraordinary success with which God blessed his ministry both in his parish and beyond it. He suffered much and he labored hard; putting most men to shame. For no less than four and twenty years he preached on an average ten or twelve sermons, and travelled a hundred miles per week. There were indeed giants on the earth in those days. He did not labor in vain in the Lord. Shining a star of the first magnitude in the constellation of England, he was held in the highest esteem and the warmest affection by the worthies of his day. Whitefield pronounced him to be an "angel of the church." Venn, defending him from opprobrium, says, that he was "as familiar with the learned languages as with his mother tongue ; and that he could be under no temptation to court respect by itinerant preaching, for he merited and enjoyed *that* in a high degree among all ranks of the literary professors at the University." Wesley pronounces on him this high eulogium : — "Mr. Berridge appears to be one of the most simple as well as most sensible men of all whom it pleased God to employ in reviving primitive Christianity. I designed to have spent but one night with him ; but Mr. Gilbert's mistake (who sent him word I would be at Everton on Friday) obliged me to stay there another day, or multitudes of people would have been disappointed. They come now twelve or fourteen miles to hear him ; and very few come in vain. His word is with power : he speaks as plain and home as John Nelson, but with all the propriety of Mr. Romaine and the tenderness of Mr. Hervey." But the noblest testimony and best reward which Berridge received was seen in the eager, moved, and melted thousands who crowded to hear him preach, and many of whom now shine as jewels in one of the brightest crowns that is worn in heaven. An eye-witness describes the church at Everton as crowded with persons from all the country round, " the windows being filled within and without, and even the outside of the pulpit to the very top, so that Mr. Berridge seemed almost stifled." At Stafleford, Grandchester, at Driflow, Orwell, and indeed wherever he went, he was a centre round which thousands and tens of thousands gathered. All eyes fixed on him, the tears rolling over their cheeks, and many, unable to keep down the swell of their emotions, crying out, " Lord what shall we do to be saved ? " Even when nearly worn out by his gigantic labors and ardent spirit, he rose on one occasion to preach at Harlston, dejected and depressed, saying — " I am now so weak, I must leave off field-preaching "; yet there, the usual effects accompanying the word, he delivered himself with amazing energy to three thousand people. And so, from Everton as his centre, the truth radiated out to London and all the provinces round about. He sounded the Gospel abroad over all the country, and in many instances, revivals, like those of Kilsyth and Cambuslang in Scotland, distinguished, and blessed, and crowned his ministry.

Not that Berridge neglected his own parish, or had occasion to say, " they made me keeper of vineyards, and mine own vineyard have I not kept." In proof of this, and as illustrating the wit and eccentricity in which he indulged when the pen was in his hand, we may insert a letter of his to his friend and coadjutor, Lady Huntingdon. She had asked him to supply some of her chapels. His reply, in which he alludes to a minister of the name of Dyer, who with some sectaries had been sowing dissension and their peculiar views among his people, as well as among her ladyship's followers, will be found in the following letter :—

"As to myself — he says, — I am now determined not to quit my charge again in a hurry. Never do I leave my bees, though for a short space only, but at my return I find them either casting and colting, or fighting and robbing each other ; not gathering honey from every flower in God's garden, but filling the air with their buzzings, and darting out the venom of their little hearts in their fiery stings. Nay, so inflamed they often are — and a mighty little thing disturbs them — that three months' tinkling afterwards with a warming-pan will scarce hive them at last, and make them settle to work again. They are now in a mighty ferment, occasioned by the sounding brass of a Welch DYER,* who has done me the same kind office at Everton that he has done my friend at Tottenham. 'Tis pity he should have the charge of anything but *wasps ;* these he might allure into

* Rev. G. Dyer, Lecturer of St. George the Martyr.

the treacle pot and step in before them himself, but he will never fill a hive with honey." In illustration of his powers as a Barnabas, we insert the following letter written to the same lady on the death of her daughter. Although marked indeed by Berridge's peculiarities, it is full of lofty thought, and pregnant with consolation:—"My Lady—I received your letter from Brighthelmstone, and hope you will soon learn to bless your Redeemer for snatching away your daughter so speedily. Methinks I see great mercy in the suddenness of her removal, and when your bowels have done yearning for her you will see it too. O! what is she snatched from? Why, truly, from the plague of an evil heart, a wicked world, and a crafty devil—snatched from all such bitter grief as now overwhelms you—from everything that might wound her ear, afflict her eye, or pain her heart. And what is she snatched to? To a land of everlasting peace, where the voice of the turtle is ever heard, where every inhabitant can say, 'I am no more sick!' no more whim in the head, no more plague in the heart, but all full of love and full of praise; ever seeing with enraptured eyes, ever blessing with adoring hearts, that dear Lamb who has washed them in his blood, and has now made them kings and priests unto God for ever and ever. Amen. Oh, madam! What would you have? Is it not better singing in heaven, 'Worthy is the Lamb that was slain,' &c. than crying at Oathall, 'O wretched woman that I am?' Is it not better for her to go before, than to stay after you? and then to be lamenting, 'Ah my mother!' as you now lament, 'Ah my daughter!' Is it not better to have your Selina taken to heaven, than to have your heart divided between Christ and Selina? If she was a silver idol before, might she not prove a golden one afterwards? She is gone to pay a most blessed visit, and will see you again by and by, never to part more. Had she crossed the sea and gone to Ireland, you could have born it; but now she is gone to heaven 'tis almost intolerable. Wonderful strange love this. Such behavior in others would not surprise me, but I could almost beat you for it; and I am sure Selina would beat you too, if she was called back but one moment from heaven to gratify your fond desires. I cannot soothe you, and I must not flatter you. I am glad the dear creature is gone to heaven before you. Lament, if you please; but glory, glory, glory be to God, says JOHN BERRIDGE."

We cannot throw together these fragments of Berridge's life and character without mentioning, that in addition to his own labors, which have had no counterpart in our day save in the lives of James Haldane and some few such men, he employed many other laborers in the same field. He hired barns, he paid preachers, and on these and works of charity, he expended the whole proceeds of his vicarage and fellowship, the price of his family plate, and the whole of a large patrimonial fortune. He kept nothing back — he did nothing by halves — although sometimes indeed he brought himself thereby into difficulties, which however, were borne without repining, and from which, like a bee that finds honey even in bitter flowers, he drew good lessons as the following extract proves : — " Friday, July 7. — I have become acquainted with the Rev. Mr. R———, of Wakefield, and find him a sensible, pious, and experienced man. He was long intimate with Mr. Berridge of Everton, whom he represents as a deeply devoted, spiritual, and humble man ; possessing a vein of great natural humor, but of very serious manners. He gave in fact all his goods to feed the poor ; and at one period, after a long illness, he was in actual distress, not knowing where to turn for support. Whilst musing on his state, he heard a rap at the door — the postman was immediately announced with a letter, on which was charged a shilling. Mr. Berridge had not a shilling to pay for it, and would not take ; but requested the postman to take it back to the office, as he said he never wished to have any thing in his house that was not paid for ; but the postman said he would call on the morrow, and insisted on leaving it. When he opened it, he found to his great surprise a bank note for thirty pounds from John Thornton. 'Who,' said he, 'can doubt after this the existence of a particular Providence?'" If our author did not always, in correspondence and conversation, restrain the overflowings of his humor, he never kept back his money in the cause of Christ; if he said some odd, he never said mean, and he always did noble things; and offering himself to God a living sacrifice on the altar of our faith, and with himself all that he had, he went through the world and lived in the church of which he was one of the best ministers and brightest ornaments, realizing the lofty wish of Brainerd:—"O! that I were a flaming fire in the service of my God!" So much for the author. As to the book itself we may remark, that

The "Christian World Unmasked" is a work which none but John Berridge could have written—the work of an extraordinary man; like a child who is the living image of his father, it proclaims its parentage. Here, as elsewhere he preserves his own character; he always did so, whether he penned letters to noble ladies, or addressed a congregation of ten thousand peasants, or stood before the dignitaries of the church like a lion at bay, trampling the canon-law beneath his feet, and claiming on the strength of a higher authority his right to preach the gospel to every creature. The book which we introduce anew to the public, has survived the test of years—and still stands towering above things of inferior growth, like a cedar of Lebanon. Its subject is all important; in doctrine it is sound to the core; it glows with fervent piety; it exhibits a most skilful and unsparing dissection of the dead professor; while its style is so remarkable that he who could preach as Berridge has written, would hold any congregation by the ears.

No doubt a very fastidious taste may find expressions here and there to jar on its delicate nerves, which some may think it were better to have smoothed and softened. We once witnessed a scene which reconciles us to leaving these as Berridge left them, and assures us that, with the great mass of readers, these spots, if such they be, will be lost like those of the sun, in a blaze of light. Seated in the front pew of a side gallery, where we had a commanding view of the audience, it was our privilege on the occasion alluded to, to hear no common preacher. His grammar was uncommonly bad; not seldom he violated the simplest idioms of our language; and no pronunciation certainly could be more uncouth than his —yet the congregation hung upon the speaker's lips. Every eye was fixed upon him; and, apparently insensible to the existence of any defect, they sat enchained by a piety which beamed in his looks and often moulded his tones into the finest oratory; and they looked perfect delight as ever and anon from the depths of his sanctified genius there rose thoughts so heavenly and sublime as to appear amid the darkness of his reasoning like rockets blazing up to heaven, bursting in the upper skies and descending on earth in a shower of fire-balls. Our author, as the work will prove, was in many respects a very different man from the preacher I have described.

Berridge laid the hand of a giant on his subject. He brought to his discourse the reasoning powers of a strong intellect, and added the accomplishments of a great scholar to the piety of a Christian and the pathos of an orator ; and indeed we are inclined to think that naturally as it came to him, that occasionally *out-of-the-way* style of exhibiting truth, which might offend a very fastidious taste, rather helped than hindered the grand object for which he prayed and preached. He could not help doing what Richard Cecil did of design on one occasion, when he found that although he had brought a carefully prepared and polished sermon to the pulpit, his audience refused him their attention. That great preacher flung it at once aside, and after a protracted pause, astonished the still and wondering assembly by crying aloud "A man was hanged at Tyburn this morning!"—Now all were awake. With that nail he fixed every ear to the pulpit, and starting from the scaffold he struck on a path altogether new, and delivered to unflagging attention a sermon of extraordinary power. We do not love Berridge the less, but rather the more for his peculiarities—not that we would have any man imitate them—for as even beauty becomes ridiculous when a jackdaw has dressed itself in peacock's feathers, an aping of others is always offensive. Their peculiarities are like a suit of clothes which hang not well on any but the man who was measured for them ; not to say that the misfortune of imitators often lies in this, that in copying the lisp, the bur, the shrug, the broad accent, the ungainly and ungraceful attitude, they forget that their idol is not great by these, but in spite of them.

If striking peculiarities of thought and expression, however, be originalities—things not borrowed but born, as they were in Berridge—then, with God's blessing, they prove not weakness but strength, as was seen in the thousands who crowded to hear him preach, and the multitudes who fell before his bow, which, like that of Ulysses, none but himself could bend. For while to its inhabitants heaven's beauties are ever new, and familiarity breeds no indifference in them, how often is that its effect in our present imperfect state? It is with spiritual objects as with the most attractive or sublime scenes of nature. The glowing sunrise, the gleaming river, the sea roused by the storm into majesty, summer walking the earth decked in a robe of flowers, the brow of night sparkling with its countless gems —many regard these with the eyes of a brute; they stir no thought; they excite no reflection; nor call forth such exclamation as the Psalmist's —"How manifold are thy works, Lord God Almighty—in wisdom thou hast made them all!" Even so, the surpassing glories of the Gospel, the cross of Calvary, the crown of heaven, are lost on eyes which have become familiar with them from the cradle and a mother's knee; and to the terrors of the law men grow as insensible as the inhabitants of the tropics to the play of lightnings, or the tenant of a cottage within the spray of Niagara to the roar of its thousand thunders. These, although they may shake the air, and stun the ears of strangers, are unheeded or unheard by him.

If among many striking, Berridge says some strange things; if always original, he is occasionally odd; if in this book there are a few instances of the picturesque approaching the grotesque, the reader will readily excuse these for the sake of the noble piety with which the book is pervaded, the golden truths that lie imbedded in its pages, and a style and manner pre-eminently calculated to rouse the dullest attention, and break through that indifference with which familiarity encrusts the most solemn and momentous subjects. Infinitely better such a book, than faultless dulness, unobjectionable common-places, an essay from press or pulpit which is bare of beauties as of blemishes, and in which, if men find no faults, they feel, as sleepers prove, none of the interest that carries the reader over the pages of the "Christian World Unmasked."

THOMAS GUTHRIE.

FROM THE NORTH BRITISH REVIEW.

At Everton, in Bedfordshire, not far from the spot where John Bunyan had been a preacher and a prisoner, lived and labored a man not unlike him, the most amusing and most affecting original of all this school—JOHN BERRIDGE. For long a distinguished member of Clare Hall, Cambridge, and for many years studying fifteen hours a day, he had enriched his masculine understanding with all sorts of learning; and when at last he became a parish minister, he applied to his labors all the resources of a mind eminently practical, and all the vigor of a very honest one. His mind was singular. So predominant was its Saxon alkali, that poetry, sentiment, and classical allusion, whatever else came into it, was sure to be neutralized into common sense—pathetic, humorous, or practical, as the case might be; and so strong was his fancy that every idea in re-appearing sparkled into a metaphor or emblem. He thought in proverbs, and he spake in parables; that granulated salt which is so popular with the English peasantry. And though his wit ran riot in his letters and his talk, when solemnized by the sight of the great congregation and the recollection of their exigencies, it disappeared. It might still be the diamond point on the sharp arrows; but it was then too swift and subtile to be seen. The pith of piety — what keeps it living and makes it strong — is love to the Saviour. In this he always abounded. "My poor feeble heart droops when I think, write, or talk of anything but Jesus. Oh that I could get near Him, and live believingly on Him! I would walk, and talk, and sit, and eat, and rest with Him. I would have my heart always doating on Him, and find itself ever present with Him." And it was this absorbing affection which in preaching enchanced all his powers, and subdued all his hazardous propensities. When ten or fifteen thousand people were gathered on a sloping field, he would mount the pulpit after Venn or Grimshaw had vacated it. A twinkle of friendly recognition darted from some eyes, and a smile of comic welcome was exchanged by others. Perhaps a merry thought was suspected in the corner of his lips, or seen salient on the very point of his peaked and curious nose. And he gave it wing. The light-hearted laughed, and those who knew no better hoped for fun. A devout stranger might have trembled and feared that it was going off in a pious farce. But no fear of Father Berridge. He knows where he is, and how he means to end. That pleasantry was intended for a nail, and see, it has fastened every ear to the pulpit-door. And now he proceeds in homely colloquy, till the bluntest boor is delighted at his own capacity, and is prepared to agree with what he says who makes so little parade and mystery. But was not that rather a home-thrust? "Yes, but it is fact; and sure enough the man is frank and honest;" and so the blow is borne with the best smile that can be twisted out of agony. "Nay, nay, he is getting personal, and without some purpose the bolts would not fly so true." And just when the hearer's suspicion is rising, and he begins to think of retreating, barbed and burning the arrow is through him. His soul is transfixed, and his conscience is all on fire. And from the quiver gleaming to the chord these shafts of living Scripture fly so fast that in a few minutes it is all a field of slain. Such was the powerful, impact, and piercing sharpness of this great preacher's sentences — so suited to England's rustic auditories, and so divinely directed in their flight, that eloquence has seldom won such triumphs as the Gospel won with the bow of old eccentric Berridge. Strong men in the surprise of sudden self-discovery, or in the joy of marvellous deliverance, would sink to the earth powerless or convulsed; and in one year of "campaigning" it is calculated that four thousand have been awakened to the worth of their souls and a sense of sin. He published a book, "The Christian World Unmasked," in which something of his close dealing and a good deal of his drollery survive. The idea of it is, a spiritual physician prescribing for a sinner ignorant of his own malady. "Gentle reader, lend me a chair, and I will sit down and talk a little with you. Give me leave to feel your pulse. Sick, indeed, sir, very sick of a mortal disease which infects your whole mass of blood." After a good deal of altercation the patient consents to go into the matter, and submits to a survey of his life and character.

Many readers might think our physician not only racy but rude. They must remember that his practice lay among farmers and graziers and ploughmen; and if they dislike his bluntness they must remember his success.

THE

CHRISTIAN WORLD UNMASKED.

GENTLE READER:

LEND me a chair, and I will sit down and talk a little with you. If my company proves unseasonable, or my discourse unsavory, you may be relieved from both by a single cast of your eye. No longer I continue talking, than whilst you continue looking upon me. My visit will be long or short, just as you please; only while it lasts, it should be friendly. I have no flattering words to give you, nor any alms to ask of you. I am come to inquire of your health, and would ask a few questions about it.

Indeed, sir, I am a physician, was regularly bred to the business, have served more than three apprenticeships at a noted *hall* of physic, and consumed a deal of candle in lighting up a little understanding; yet am reviled as a mountebank, because I have been seen upon a stage. The Prince of physic set the fashion; and his example satisfies me, though it may not content another.

However, sir, my business does not lie with the walls of your house, but with the tenant within. I bring no advice to strengthen your clay, but wish to see your spirit healed, and to set the heavenly lamp a burning. Give me leave to feel your pulse :—— sick indeed, sir; very sick; and of a mortal disease, received from your parents, and which infects your whole mass of blood. *There is no health in you;* and since you seem not sensible of the malady, I must pronounce you delirious.

Why, you frighten me, doctor. Sure you was bred at Sion College, along with Doctor Whitefield and his brethren. A very hard mouthed race truly! Who have dealt so much in severe remedies, no genteel people will employ them. Their practice lieth chiefly among the poor, who can bear banging.

However, since you are come upon a friendly visit, I will tell you honestly what I think of myself. I have my faults, as well as my neighbors; but my appetites are pretty well bridled. My heart is honest, quite willing to pay all men their due; my hands, too, are sometimes disposed to relieve a neighbor's want; and my feet go orderly to church on a Sunday, when the bells chime, except it proves a rainy day; and then I read the weekly paper, or a bible chapter at home, just as suits my fancy. This I call a regular life, and it is the ground of my hope; not forgetting Jesus Christ, to help out some defects. For I am choleric, no doubt; but it quickly bloweth over; and a little apt to fib in a market, but who can help it? All my neighbors do the same; and my landlord, who talks much of his honor, will tell a fib upon occasion, as well as myself. Now, from these circumstances, it should seem that I am not mortally sick as you suppose, but enjoy good christian health. Yet I do not like your countenance, it looks so very cloudy. Are you in pain, Doctor?

No, sir, but I am sadly grieved at the weak account you have given of yourself. It convinces me you are not sick, but dead — dead to God, and to his spiritual service. I expected some account of a *true Christian*, and you put me off with the state of a *poor heathen*, who is somewhat sober and honest and charitable, and worships his God when the weather suits, or his inclination serves. I find no trace of a spiritual mind, no taste of a gospel blessing, no earnest of a future inheritance. God's word, I see, is not your sweet companion; his service not your true delight; his glory not your noble aim. Your religion floats upon the surface, like froth upon the water, and is a mere vanity. God has yet no hold of your heart, and you cannot give it him.

If you were a *child of God*, his Spirit would instruct you to love and reverence him with the affections of a child; and by prayer to converse with him daily, as children converse with their parents.

If God were your Father, you would love his house. It would be dear unto you; and a little rain would no more keep you from his courts, than from a fair or market. Where should a child go but to his Father's house? And if a child of God, you would say, as David did, *How lovely is thy dwelling-place, O Lord! A day in thy courts is better than a thousand.*

If you were a *real subject* of Christ, the kingdom, which you ask for, in his short prayer, would come, and be set up within you — a kingdom of *righteousness, peace and joy in the Holy Ghost.* He would enable you, not only to profess him, but to love and serve him, and fix your *whole* dependence upon him. Your bosom would become his presence-chamber, where he would *manifest himself to you, as he does not to the world:* and your heart would be his throne, where he would sit, to sanctify your affections, to regulate your tempers, and subdue you to himself.

Jesus Christ is not a pasteboard king, with royal titles but without authority. He sits upon his holy hill, invested with all power, to captivate the hearts of his subjects, and execute his threatened vengeance on his adversaries. And where he brings men under the sway of his sceptre, he bestows the blessings of his kingdom. The Holy Spirit, as a *comforter*, is granted: the *peace, passing all understanding, is given:* and *God's love is shed abroad in the heart by the Holy Ghost.* These jewels are dug only out of gospel mines, and set only in the breast of gospel subjects. And where they are well set, Jesus Christ becomes exceeding dear to such. They know the purchase-price he paid, and, having tasted of the blessings, they love his person, and adore his grace. Paul and they are now agreed, to *know only Jesus Christ, and him crucified.* He is their song and boast, their peace and hope, their all in all.

Let me draw my chair a little closer, sir: plain dealing is exceeding needful here. If you are not a *real subject* of Jesus Christ, you must be a stranger to the blessings of his kingdom. The jewels I have mentioned are not locked up in your cabinet; they are not bestowed upon the outward court worshippers. You must come within the vail, which is now rent open for access, before you can view a reconciled Father, and feast upon his grace.

A decent walk will keep you from mistrusting your condition; and these heavenly comforts may be thought too rich for a state of pilgrimage; and the remnant, who possess them, may be deemed a little brain-sick, quite unworthy of your notice. Perhaps the first Christians may have tasted of these blessings; but you think the gospel wine, which was broached at first, is now run out, and nothing left for us to sip but the lees. Thus you are fortified in the castle of security; your conscience, when it cries, is rocked fast asleep; and with the mask of a decent profession, you live a stranger to Christ's kingdom, and perish in your sins.

Nay, sir, do not start away, but keep your seat and give my words a little hearing. Let your conscience speak; it has an honest voice, though a coarse one; and if you cannot bear handling, it is a sign that you have ugly sores within, which are not less dangerous from being skinned over. I must probe again, to make you feel the sores; and if my master guide my hand, I shall reach the quick, and hear you cry, as a perfect man of old did, *Behold I am vile!*

Whilst you remain a stranger to Christ's inward kingdom, you are, with all your outward decency, but a painted tomb, full of all uncleanness. And because the walls of your house have had a white-wash, and hide its inward filth, and keep it secret from your fellow creatures, you care not much about that eye of God, which views your heart, and views it with abhorrence. Your bosom is a *cage of unclean birds*, and you dearly love their chirping, and feed them with your own hand. In this retired chamber you riot in uncleanness, and if your filthy thoughts were all exposed to the world, you would almost die with shame. And yet perhaps so void of shame, as to think yourself a chaste person, if no outward acts of uncleanness are committed. Oh, sir, how can your heart, your filthy heart, appear before God—an holy God? Do you read the Bible? There I find it written, *Blessed are the pure in heart, for they shall see God.* You are satisfied with *clean hands*, a decent profession; but God requires a *clean heart*, and none shall see his face without it.

But, sir, your breast is a *den of thieves* too, where self-will and self-sufficiency, the *head* of the gang, are up in arms against God, rejecting his authority, breaking down his fences, and laying his enclosures common; a den where anger, envy, pride, railing, lying, discontent, and worldliness, the *tail* of the gang, have stripped your bosom of its heavenly furniture, and turned God's ancient house into a market, worse than Billingsgate. What was God's court is now a den, where distraction lifts her clamorous voice, and violence deals her heavy hand. So that a man's worst foes are they of his own house, the thieves that lodge within his breast.

Sir, if Jesus Christ kept his court in your bosom, he would make peace there; for he is the Prince of Peace. Where he reigns he does command peace, for the honor of his name as Saviour, and for the glory of his government as King. But how can you suppose that Christ is your King, when he lets your house be daily rifled by a gang of thieves? A gracious prince will not endure to see his subjects ravaged daily when he has sufficient power to protect them.

And with what conscience can you call yourself a subject of Christ Jesus, when your bosom is a sturdy rebel, and content to be so? You might as well call me your prince, as Jesus Christ your King, if he does not rule within your breast; and might as properly call me your Maker, as Christ your Saviour, if he does not save you from your sins. Where he rules as King, and shews himself a Saviour, he will purge the conscience by his blood from guilt, and hallow well the heart by his Spirit. He will cleanse the *cage*, and scour the *den;* and when a wanton bird presumes to chirp, he will wring its neck off; or if a rogue assault your house, his palace, he will apprehend the thief, and sentence him to Tyburn. Nay, it is a fixed rule with him, that whoever harbors thieves, shall have his house pulled down, and a dreadful fire set to it, which burns and never will be quenched.

If my expressions ever wear an air of pleasantry, it is because I would tempt you to hear me out. My subject is weighty, but may seem too grave, as the modern taste goes, without a little seasoning. Well, sir, what think you of yourself? Are you a real subject of Jesus Christ, or an alien?

Indeed, doctor, more is lacking in me than I thought. I have been resting on a decent conduct and my Sunday prayers; but something still, I find, is wanting; and the main thing too. The house which I have built, seemed a creditable house, and was thought to be as good as the vicar's; for we build exactly with the same materials. But I perceive, at length, there are no windows in the house, nor any furniture in the chambers. And no wonder if a dark house becomes a den of thieves, for they love the night, and dwell in darkness. However, I am now provided with some light for the windows, and must seek out furniture for the chambers. I would not willingly miscarry in this matter, because it is of moment. And it would be sad indeed, after building and repairing all my days, to have the house upon my head at last. But I trust by the help of a *good-will* and a *lusty arm* of my own, to fray the birds away, dislodge the gang, and furnish well my house. What think you now, doctor? Do I not talk like a man?

Yes, sir, very much like an heathen man, but not at all like a Christian. You speak with a right Canaanitish boast; but Canaanites, though giants, were overcome and slain. If you find no better help than your own will and your own arm, your house will be down at last, and bury you in its ruins.

Men are strangers to the spiritual nature of God's law, and to the woful depravity of the human heart, and therefore entertain a meagre notion of religion, and a lofty thought of their own ability. If christian faith is nothing but a mere assent to the gospel-word, every man may make himself a true believer when he please. And if christian duty does consist in Sunday-service only, with a pittance of sobriety, and honesty, and charity, we might expect that men would vaunt of will and power to make themselves religious. And yet the generality are much defective here. They often talk of turning over new leaves; but their future life proves such talk is empty boast, and that they want a will and power for this slender reformation. All allow that nothing is more needful to be done; and nothing can account for its being left undone, but a want of human will and strength to do it.

Let me step into your closet, sir, and peep upon its

furniture. My hands are pretty honest, you may trust me; and nothing will be found, I fear, to tempt a man to be a thief. — Well, to be sure, what a filthy closet is here! Never swept, for certain, since you was christened? And what a fat idol stands skulking in the corner! A sweet heart-sin, I warrant it. How it simpers, and seems as pleasant as a right eye. Can you find a *will* to part with it, or *strength* to pluck it out? And supposing you a match for this self-denial; can you so command your heart as to *hate* the sin you do forsake? This is certainly required. Truth is called for in the inward parts. God will have sin not only cast aside, but cast away with abhorrence. So he speaks; *Ye that love the Lord, hate evil.*

It is easy to affirm we have ability for this, and then dispute about it eagerly; yet who makes the trial? I have made it many times, and find I can do nothing to good purpose. Others seem well satisfied, with supposing they have power, but make no thorough trial. Else they would find, and would confess, they can effectually do nothing.

If the wanton nightingale is put out of your *cage* on a Sunday morning, she will be taken in again at night. Your heart will pine for her midnight whistle, and cannot hate her note, or think it half so horrid as the hissing of a serpent, or the croaking of a toad, though far more loathsome than both.

Can you find a pleasant heart to *love your enemies, and pray for them, and do them good?* Perhaps you may compel yourself to show them kindness; and this is sooner said than done. Yet *shewing* kindness to an enemy is one thing, and *feeling* kindness for them is another; and both are *equally* required. Pray, make a trial here of your boasted will and power; and see if they do not prove of brittle metal, and snap between your fingers.

You own yourself a mortal man, notwithstanding all your mighty strength, and expect a mansion in the skies when you quit this house of clay. But, sir, you must be taught the work of heaven, before you can be settled there. An earthly heart could no more live in heaven than a fish upon dry land. The element is too fine for both. It makes them sick; they cannot breathe in such an atmosphere.

Grace is blossom-bud of glory; and a work of grace upon the heart is a needful preparation for glory. By grace men are brought into the school of Christ, and bound apprentices for heaven. In this school they learn to *walk with God, to love him, and to serve him — to be strangers upon earth, and seek a better country; looking for the coming of the Son of God.* These are some Scripture marks of the heirs of glory. Do you find them in your breast; or can you stamp them there? Indeed you cannot. None but he who turned water into wine can change your earthly nature to an heavenly. You must be born from above before you learn to crave, and truly seek the things above. You may peruse the word of God, but can you say with David, *Lord, how I love thy law! it is my meditation all the day?*

When a bible and newspaper are found upon your table, I can guess which your hand will take up first; and you know the heart directs the hand. The worldly magazine is sweeter to your taste than the heavenly leaves. You may force and drive your thoughts on heavenly things; but can you set your heart upon them? If so, your thoughts and talk would glide on heavenly things most pleasantly; for *out of the abundance of the heart the mouth speaketh.*

But, is this your case; or the case of others who are reckoned decent people? You know it is not. They have no *liking* for religious subjects, and find no *power* to introduce them. Conversation turns upon the earth, because the heart is earthly. Religious talk is unfashionable, because it is unsuitable to our fallen nature. We do not care to think or talk of God, our daily benefactor, because we are not born of God, and have no filial kindness for him. His blessings are received daily, and the author most politely is forgotten. No mention must be made of him, who gave us all we have, and keeps us what we are. To talk of God upon a visit, would turn the hearers sick or sour, and brand the speaker for a rude man and a methodist. All ingratitude is reckoned infamous, except ingratitude to God. Such is human nature, and the *kind* religion of it.

What makes the curate give you such a scanty sermon, just the fag-end of a subject? And what makes the people love to have it so? The reason, sir, is plain. A Sunday dinner is more savory than the word of God.

But, sir, if your house is furnished, as you threaten, then your parlor, shop, and closet must be lined with devotion: this is christian furniture. Can you pray, and find sweet fellowship with God in prayer? You talk of will and power: if they are at hand, why are they not in exercise? I call that man a boaster, and suspect his poverty, who talketh of his riches, yet never pays his debts. No work is more needful, more profitable, or more honorable than prayer; and when rightly performed, none is more delightful. Why then is it not more followed? Indeed, sir, you have no heart to pray, till *God poureth out a spirit of grace and supplication on you.* You may force your lips to *say* a prayer, and say it often, but cannot force your heart to like it. The work is irksome — mighty irksome. It drags on heavily like a jaded mill-horse who is whipped round and round, but longs to be released from his gears. A manger suits him better than a collar.

And can God be pleased with that service which your own heart loatheth? No, sir; he requires a cheerful service; the obedience of sons, and not of slaves. He says, *Give me thy heart;* and his people are a *willing people*— made willing by his grace.

But supposing that a little *will* for prayer might be squeezed from a flinty heart, you have no *power* still to compass fellowship with God. And what is prayer without divine communion? A mere prating to a dead wall or blue sky. It is babbling to an unknown God, as four hundred and fifty prophets did to Baal, a jolly company, from morning till evening, but *found no answer.* Baal kept no fellowship with his votaries then, and never has done since.

Praying unto God without communion, is like talking to a man, who neither gives an answer, nor a smile, nor yet a look. You would soon be weary of such converse, and avoid such company. And no people find an heart to pray, who feel no fellowship with God.

You often hear at church, St. Paul's parting prayer, "The grace of our Lord Jesus Christ, and the love of God, and the *fellowship of the Holy Ghost*, be with you." By nature we are far from God; sin has made the separation. And till brought nigh to him, we cannot say with them of old, *We have fellowship with the Father, and with his son Jesus Christ.* It is one office of the Holy Spirit to draw our spirit near to God, and give us fellowship with him.

This fellowship is not obtained by a mere *profession* of the gospel, however decent that profession is, but by *regeneration* or a spiritual birth. Where the Holy Spirit has imparted spiritual life, he instructs a sinner how to pray, helps his infirmities in praying, draws the human spirit nigh to God, and gives communion with him. Thus the heart is strengthened and refreshed by prayer, and finds it both a pleasant and a profitable service. But where communion is not felt, nor truly sought, no comfort can be found in prayer, nor profit. And this is much the case of modern Christianity — a dull, insipid thing, void of *spiritual life*, and therefore void of *spiritual feeling*. Professors do not make pretence unto it, but disclaim it. So far, indeed, they are honest; but being destitute of spiritual life and feeling, they must be called gospel-puppets, danced with devotional wires. A church is fitted up for their stage, with boxes, pit, and gallery; and Sunday is the day of acting. During the performance, some are mighty decent characters, like a king and queen of France; others rude and racketty, like cobbler Punch and his wife.

Yet further, men have no heart to pray, because they

have no *feeling* of their wants. If I am, or fancy that I am, endowed with will and power to help myself, it seems a needless thing to beg of God to give me grace — as needless as to ask his help to light my candle. And where men boast of native strength, I do suppose they act consistently, and seldom chafe a knee in prayer. Common decency requires a little outward homage, and a little will suffice.

Now, sir, be pleased to hear what my dispensatory says concerning will and power. *It is God who worketh in you, both to will and do;* and he works the will and power, not for our desert, but merely *of his own good pleasure.* God stands in debt to none; and his works are not designed to reward man's merit, but to manifest his glorious grace.

When your will is turned from evil, or inclined to good, it is the Lord's doing. He overrules the will, though not asked of him, nor perceived by you. This may be gathered from the text above cited, and is confirmed by the following story: —

Abraham comes to Gerar, and through fear denies his wife. Abimelech sends for Sarah to his house, purposing to take her to his bed; but when she comes, he is somehow wholly overruled. God appears to Abimelech in a dream, and says, *Thou art a dead man, for the woman thou hast taken is a man's wife.* Abimelech protests *his heart is upright, and his hands are innocent.* God allows it, and says *I know thou hast done this in the integrity of thine heart;* but then he shews the cause of this integrity — *For* I withheld *thee from sinning against me; therefore* I suffered thee not *to touch her.* In Abimelech we behold the doctrine of nature. He vaunts of his integrity, as modern Christians do; and is just as ignorant of God's determining his will, and of course as unthankful for that determination, as modern Christians are. We need not wonder at it. Nature is the same at all times, and in all dispensations. Grace alone makes the difference.

Hence real Christians learn to seek for will and power from God; and give him hearty praise for all escapes from evil; and for every good desire wrought in them, and for all good works performed by them. As for you, sir, and others, who can turn yourselves round by your own will and power as nimbly as a floating weathercock, I wish the weeping prophet's prayer was much upon your lips — *Turn thou me, O Lord, and so shall I be turned.*

But, sir, you call yourself an honest man, and honest men will pay their debts. You own yourself a sinner too, and sins are debts due to God. How are these debts to be discharged? They are a most enormous sum; and, when felt, will prove a heavy load; and if not cancelled, must bring on eternal ruin. Do you think of this matter, sir? It is a weighty business.

Yes, yes, doctor, I have had some thoughts about it, and do not apprehend much danger or much trouble here. I must *repent*, and *amend*, and do what I *can*, and Christ will do the rest. Some debts I shall pay myself, a *decent* part of the work, and Jesus must discharge the rest of the reckoning. This is our parish way of paying sinful debts, and seems a very good way. We desire no better, and only wish to pay our neighbor's debts as easily. What think you of it, doctor? sure you can have no objection here.

Indeed, sir, this way of paying sinful debts, as easy as it seems to you, would ruin me effectually. *The wages of sin is death ;* and if I must pay off only one sin, I am ruined ; for that debt is death. So of course I die, and perish. No help is found for me in this way. Either I must be forgiven wholly, or wholly be undone.

This method of payment would make you a bankrupt presently, and ruin you eternally. Pray, examine it a little closer. First, you talk of *repenting.* True ; repentance goes before forgiveness. But you speak as if repentance was your own work ; whereas the Bible says, it is the *gift of God ;* and Jesus is exalted up on high *to give it.* You had better pray for repentance, than try to squeeze it from a mill-stone; and such is every heart by nature. No kind of relenting is found there till Jesus sends it. What your own hands bestow can avail you nothing, but will need to be repented of. And where God gives repentance, it is never meant to purchase pardon. For tears pay no debts. They will not pay your neighbors' ; and much less God's, which are weighty debts indeed.

Repentance is designed to make the heart loathe sin, through a sense of its deep pollution ; and dread sin through a feeling of its guilty burden. Thus the heart becomes acquainted with its nakedness and ruin, is broken down and humbled, and forced to fly to Jesus Christ, and seek deliverance by grace *alone.* Nor is the business quickly done. When the heart is conscious of its misery, it will try a thousand legal tricks to shake it off: but, wearied out at length with endless disappointment, it falls at Jesus' feet, and meekly takes up Peter's prayer — *Lord, save, or I perish.*

After repenting, you talk of *amending*. Ay, to be sure. No repentance can be true without amendment. But you seem to think your heart only wants amending, and may be mended just as easy as your coat. Truly, sir, it wants new making; and no real mending can be found without new making. All the rest is varnish, which may please yourself, and satisfy a neighbor, but will not content your God. A blackmoor, painted white, is but a blackmoor still; an emblem of a decent modern Christian. Your conduct may be much reformed; but your heart, unless created new, will be full of earthliness and all uncleanness, and remain the devil's forge and work-shop still. No thorough change is made until the work begins from above, and God creates the heart anew. When repentance is bestowed, David's prayer will suit you well — *Create in me a clean heart, and renew a right spirit in me.*

But supposing God should bless you with a *new heart* and *right spirit, and thereby cause you to walk in his statutes* — still, I ask what becomes of past arrears? No compensation yet is made for former trespasses. Doing present duty cannot pay old past debts. Yet these debts must be discharged, or you are ruined; and you have no overplus to pay a single debt. Nay, you are running deeper into debt daily, by doing what you ought not, and leaving undone what you ought to do. Still your deserved wages every day and every hour is death. Let me remind you once again of Peter's prayer — *Lord, save, or I perish.*

Lastly, you say I must do what I *can* and Christ will do the rest. This is the common cry, the general run; and is thought a safe and easy passage for a Christian.

But the passage is too strait and hazardous for me. I dare not venture my own soul upon it. Supposing you have will and power for duty, then I ask, Do you pray as much as you *can*, or read the Scriptures as much as you *can*, or relieve the poor as much as you *can*, or visit the sick as much as you *can?* Do you deny yourself as much as you *can;* and watch against sin as much as you *can;* or do any one duty as much as you *can?* Indeed you do not, and you know you do not. But if you put salvation on this footing, of doing what you *can*, and have not done it, what sentence can you look for from the Lord, but this? *Out of thy own mouth I will judge thee.*

If this plea, of doing what you *can*, will not abide a trial, no other plea remains but doing what you *will*, or what you *please*, and making Jesus Christ do all the rest. But you dare not urge this plea. It is too shameful and barefaced for any mortal to avow it. Now, sir, if you are not able to abide the trial of doing what you *can*, and dare not urge the shameful plea of doing what you *will*, how is it possible for you to be saved by your doings? Either a full pardon and a free salvation must be granted through Jesus Christ *alone*, or you are *undone* by your *doings*, cast and lost for ever.

Perhaps you think that Christ came to shorten man's duty, and make it more feasible, by shoving a commandment out of Moses' tables, as the papists have done; or by clipping and paring all the commandments, as the moralists do. Thus *sincere* obedience, instead of *perfect*, is now considered as the law of works.

But, sir, if Jesus Christ came to shorten man's duty, he came to give us a license to sin. For duty cannot be shortened without breaking commandments. And thus

Christ becomes a minister of sin with a witness, and must be ranked at the head of antinomian preachers.

And what do you mean by *sincere* obedience? It is a pretty expression, and serves many pretty purposes. It has so vague a meaning, it will signify anything or nothing, just as you please. It is Satan's catch-word for the gospel; and upon his gates might be truly written, *Room for sincere obedience.*

But what is it? If sincere obedience means anything, it must signify either doing what you *can*, or doing what you *will.* So we are got upon the old swampy ground again, are sinking apace into a quagmire, and shall be strangled presently, unless we retire.

Jesus Christ is so far from intending to pare away Moses' tables, that he carries every commandment to its utmost extent. A wanton look is declared to be adultery; and a wrathful heart is deemed murder; and the man who calls his neighbor a fool is threatened with hell-fire. This does not look like shortening man's duty, and making it sit more easy on a squeamish stomach. Surely this preaching cries out mainly against sincere obedience — a doctrine sweetly framed to set the heavenly gates wide open for the worst of men.

Jesus says expressly, that *he did not come to destroy the law*, by weakening or shortening Moses' tables; and he assures us, that whoever shall break the *least* commandment, and teach men to do so, shall be *least* in the kingdom of heaven, or farthest from it.

If another witness is needful, we may call in St. James, who is just at hand, and a favorite with the champions for works and sincere obedience. But the good apostle happens to be rather sturdy in this matter, and declares that if *a man should keep the whole law, except in one point, he is yet guilty of all.* A failure in a single article ruins him. Whoever breaks the least command, or neglects the least duty, thereby procures to himself as solid a title to eternal misery, as the man who breaks all the commandments every day of his life—which is designed to show the absolute impossibility of being justified in any manner by our works.

Why, doctor, you amaze me mightily. I never heard such language in my life before. Our parish doctor does not treat his patients in this rough manner. Surely you have overshot the mark. What is really just and equitable among men, will be just and equitable with God. And is anything found among men that bears a resemblance to this proceeding of God ?

Yes, sir, enough is found in every country, and in your own land, to justify God herein. Many crimes are punished with death in Britain, and the punishment is inflicted for a *single* crime. The law does not inquire, whether you have offended *often*, but whether you have offended *once*. It tries you for a *single* offence ; and if found guilty, will condemn you without mercy. Now if human laws are not taxed with injustice, though they doom a man to die for a *single* act of treason, murder, robbery, or forgery, why should God's law be thought unjust because it punishes a single crime with death ?

However, you must not mistake St. James' meaning. He does affirm that a single breach of God's law deserves eternal death, as well as ten thousand ; yet he does not say, that small and great offenders will have equal punishment. No; mighty sinners will be mightly tormented. Men's future torment will be suited to the number and the greatness of their crimes. Yet moderate offenders can have small consolation from hence, because the shorest punishment is eternal, and the coldest place in hell will prove a hot one.

Sir, by your countenance, I perceive you are not yet disposed to renounce sincere obedience. And, though unable to maintain your ground, you are not willing to give up your arms, and ask our noble *Captain* quarter, to save your life. Let the matter take a little more sifting. You seemed to complain of God for making death the wages of a single sin; but you might have reason to complain, if God had made sincere obedience a *condition* of salvation, because no man understands what it means. Much talked of it is, like the good man in the moon, yet none could ever ken it. I dare defy the scribes and all the lawyers in the world, to tell me truly what sincere obedience is; whether it means the doing half my duty, or three quarters, or one quarter, or one fiftieth, or one hundredth part. Where must we draw the line of sincere obedience? It surely needs a magic wand to draw it. And can we think that God would leave a matter of such moment at such dreadful hazard? Whatever is made a *condition* in a human or divine covenant, be that condition less or more, sincere or perfect obedience, it must be executed punctually, from first to last, or the covenant is forfeited. On this account, conditions in a covenant always are and must be marked out precisely. Yet here, sincere obedience is called a condition, and no one knows what it is, nor will allow this poor unmeaning thing, whatever it is, to be absolutely binding. It is a condition and no condition; just as much grace as you choose, and as many or as as few good works as you please. O, fine condition! Surely Satan was the author of it.

When human lawgivers judge a crime deserveth death, and make it capital, they always draw the line of death, and mark the crime exactly, that all may know what it is, and when they do commit it. And if God hath made sincere obedience the *condition* of salvation, he would certainly have drawn the line, and marked out the boundary precisely, because our life depended on it.

If some Utopian prince should frame a body of laws, and declare that every one, who did not keep the laws *sincerely* as well as ever he could, should die, this pleasant sanction would make a dull Bæotian grin; and when the judges took a circuit in this fairy land, each assize would prove a maiden one, no doubt. Now if such a constitution would be hooted at among men, as the utmost foolishness of folly, can we think the wise God would adopt such a system?

Sincere obedience is called the condition of salvation; but God has drawn no line to mark the boundary; therefore every man must draw the line for himself. Now, sir, observe the consequence. Mark how this ravelled clew winds up, and shews its filthy bottom. One prays on Sundays, but no other time—that is his line of devotion. Another prays only in a tempest—that is his line. And a third will pray only when sick or dying. One is mellow once a week, and staggers home, but keeps upon his legs—that is his line of sobriety. Another gets much tipsy every night, but drinks no spirituous liquors — that is his line. And a third will take a dram stoutly, but declares *sincerely* that he *cannot* help it: he should be dead without it. What must we say to these things? They are all condemned. But if God has drawn no boundary, man must draw it, and will draw it, where he pleaseth. Sincere obedience thus becomes a nose of wax: and is so fingered, as to fit exactly every human face. I look upon this doctrine as the devil's master-piece, the most ingenious trap that ever was contrived by him. Where other woful doctrines slay a thousand, this will slay ten thousand. Talking of sincere obedience, and of doing what we can, is mighty plausible. It sounds well, and looks decent; but opens a dreadful sluice for the profligate, and erects a noble pillar for the deist.

I cannot think that the growth of deism is chiefly owing to the growth of immorality. A person will not surely choose to be a deist because he grows more wicked. He will not merely reject Jesus Christ because he stands in more need of him. But a man becomes a deist by hearing of sincere obedience, and believing there is merit in it. Now the price of merit is not fixed in a Protestant market. It is much talked of, but not *rated*. He therefore sets what price he pleaseth on his own merit; and pays his heavy debts off, as a neighbouring state once did, by raising the currency of its coin. Thus, though he may have been enormously wicked, yet by the fancied merit of a few good works in life, or by a charitable sum bequeathed at his death, he goes in a fiery chariot up to heaven, unless he chance to be kidnapped in the way by Satan.

If works are a *condition* in the gospel-covenant, then

works must make the *whole* of it. Sincere obedience, as a condition, will lead you unavoidably up to *perfect* obedience. No intermediate point can be assigned where you may stop. All the commands of God are enforced by the same authority. He that saith, *Commit no adultery,* saith also, *Do not kill.* And if you allow *one* duty to be absolutely binding, you must allow *all* the rest. For they all stand upon the same footing.

But perhaps you think, though all the commands of God are binding, they bind only to a *certain degree;* and hence the gospel-covenant is called a covenant of grace. Then I ask, sir, what is *that degree?* How far *must* we go, and where *may* we stop? You cannot mark the limit, and God does assign none. Yet if this had been the tenor of the gospel-covenant, he would have marked *that degree* precisely, because my life depended upon knowing it.

What saith your bible? How readest thou? Does it allow you to be guilty of adultery, or murder, or blasphemy, or perjury, or theft to a *certain degree?* Indeed it does not. Or may you indulge a *measure* of anger, or envy, or malice, or lying? Indeed you may not. My testament says, *Put away from you* all *bitterness, and wrath, and anger, and clamor, and evil-speaking, with* all *malice.* And it commands you not only to abstain from evil, but from all *appearance* of it.

Thus you can neither exclude *any kind* of duty, nor *any degree* of each kind. But the moment you seek to be justified in any measure by obedience, that moment you *fall from grace,* and *become a debtor to do the whole law.*

God has proposed no more than two covenants. The

first was *wholly* of works, which says, *do* and *live;* and gives the man a title unto life, who shall keep the law perfectly. The second covenant is *wholly* of grace, which says, *believe* and be *saved.* In this covenant salvation is *fully purchased* by Jesus Christ, and *freely applied* to the sinner by his Spirit. Grace lays the foundation, and grace brings forth the top-stone with shouting. Glory be to God for this grace.

Now the first covenant is allowed on all hands to be *too hard,* and the second is thought by most to be *too easy,* and would fall to pieces unless shored up by sincere obedience. Accordingly, by the help of this rotten buttress, men have patched up a third covenant, consisting *partly* of works and *partly* of grace, in which the sinner owns himself indebted something, he knows not what, to Jesus Christ; and takes the rest, be what it will, to himself. The captain and the soldier make a joint purse, and purchase a crown between them. The soldier wins some gold to make the crown, and Jesus studs it round with diamonds. Oh, rare soldier! He must not ascribe *salvation unto God and the Lamb, as the saints* do, but to the *Lamb* and the *soldier.*

The mixed covenant is the darling of nature. It both cherishes our vanity, and opens a door for licentiousness. The judaizing Christians, mentioned in the Acts, were the first who began to adulterate the Gospel, by blending the covenants, and seeking to be justified by faith and works conjointly. They did not consider the precepts of the Gospel as a *rule* of life, but as a *bond* of the covenant. And they were led into this error, partly by a *constitutional pride* which is common to all; and partly by a *national prejudice* which was peculiar to themselves. Moses had been their lawgiver, and works were the letter of his covenant. Of course they would be tenacious of a law of works, and as unwilling to give up their old lawgiver as an husband is to part with the wife of his youth. Moses had reigned long over them, and they gloried in being his disciples; but Jesus now would be their king. And like a besieged people, who are driven to the last extremity if they cannot keep the conqueror out, they will make the best terms they can for themselves and their prince. If Moses must not reign alone, he shall be seated near the conqueror, and they will swear fealty to both.

Wherever these judaizing Christians came and found men disposed, as they are naturally, for the mixed covenant, they always preached circumcision to them, saying, *Except ye be circumcised, ye cannot be saved.* And they preached right, if the Gospel be a mixed covenant of faith and works.

No, doctor, hold there; more words than one to this bargain. You may tàlk as you please, but I will not be circumcised; no, verily, not I. What a fine figure I should make at church! How my neighbors all would stare and point at me! and how the vicar too would jeer! I desire to hear no more of circumcision; and the thought of your pruning knife so bewilders me, that I have dropt all the ends of your discourse about sincere obedience. Could you pick the threads up again, and wrap them in a little compass?

But to return to our subject; sincere obedience is nowhere mentioned in the gospel as a *condition* of salvation. If it were a condition, sure it would have been *expressly* mentioned, because of its high importance. Yet the bible is not only silent in this matter, but asserts the contrary. St. Paul declares roundly, *We are saved by grace through faith: not of works, lest any man should boast.* The reason added, *Lest any man should boast,* plainly shuts out all works of sincere obedience as a *condition.* For though these works are often small enough, yet if the condition is fulfilled by them, such is human vanity, they would afford a ground for boasting. Therefore to dig the whole cankered root of merit up, and give all the glory of *salvation unto God and the Lamb,* the apostle says absolutely, *It is of grace; not of works.* Works have no share in the covenant of grace, as a *condition* of life. They are only the *fruit* of salvation freely bestowed, and the *genuine evidence* of a true faith, which *works* by love.

Again, if because obedience is inculcated in the covenant of grace, it is thought to be required as a *condition* of salvation; and, though not mentioned expressly, is certainly intended. Then I ask what is the condition? It is highly needful for me to know it, and to know it perfectly, because my life depends upon it. I suppose sincere obedience must mean something *short* of perfect. Pray, sir, how *much short?* Half an inch, or half a mile? Where must I draw my line, and fix my staff? The Bible has not told me, and you cannot tell me, nor all the scribes in Christendom. So I am brought to a fine pass! Here my life depends on a condition which must be performed, and I know nothing of it, nor can know, and yet am ruined if I take a step too short. Oh, sir, if sincere obedience had been a condition of salvation, God would certainly have shown me how much short it comes of per-feet; and have marked out the line exactly, whither I must go, and where I might stop.

Further, you describe sincere obedience by doing what you *can;* and thus explain one loose expression by another full as loose. I call the expression *loose*, not merely for its loose meaning, but for its loose tendency. And here we may behold the subtlety of Satan, who blinds our eyes with such expressions as bear a *decent* countenance, and *seem* to have a meaning, yet leave us wholly in the dark, or leave us at full liberty to put any soft construction on them. Yet if men were honest, they might see that doing what they *can*, means nothing more in plain English than doing what they *will;* and if they are tried by the rule of doing what they *can*, they must be all condemned, because they daily do such things as they need not and ought not, and leave undone other things which they might do and ought to do.

Here it may be noted that what is called by plain men *sincere obedience* is entitled by the scribes a *remedial law*, or the *law of love*. They are all cankered branches from the same cankered stock; and their number is convenient. A troop looks well. They serve as pretty loopholes, to play at hide-and-seek in. No wonder that the foot is often shifted, when the ground is miry. Men will make an hundred *kind* of *laws*, but God has only *two*, the *law of works*, and the *law of faith*. And what has been urged against sincere obedience equally affects a remedial law, the law of love, and all their Jewish kindred. They must stand, or fall together.

Lastly, sincere obedience, as a condition, can terminate only in perfect obedience. No middle point can be assigned where you may stop. *No kind* of duty can be excluded, nor *any degree* of each kind. Thus you are unavoidably thrust upon a perfect law of works, and *become a debtor to the whole law*. And if you dare not rest on a perfect obedience, unceasingly performed from the first day to the last, there is no other resting for you but on Jesus Christ *alone*. He must be your all; and he will be your all, or nothing.

Thus I have gathered up my ends respecting this matter; and I trust you see at length that sincere obedience is nothing but a jack-o'-lanthorn, dancing here and there and everywhere. No man could ever catch him, but thousands have been lost by following him. A cripple might as well rest upon his shadow for support, as your heart depend upon the phantom of sincere obedience.

Your mixed covenant is a mere bubble, blown up by the breath of pride. It has neither a foot in heaven, nor a foot on earth, but is pendulous in the air, and rests upon a castle floating in the clouds, which threatens downfall and ruin every moment. Woe be to the man that is seated on it. Yet this castle, though the baseless fabric of a vision, is the glory of a modern Christian; and, being built upon the clouds, has been reckoned safe from gun-shot. But I trust the cloud is burst, and the phantom disappears.

Indeed, doctor, I begin to perceive my old sweetheart, *sincere obedience*, is a very sorry hussey. Yet her face is so plausible, and her speech so winning, none would suspect her for a jilt. She must be packed off; but what shall I do when she is turned out of doors? You have jostled me out of my easy chair, and now I have not got a stool to sit upon. My obedience will afford *no sort of title* unto heaven. Where then must I find a title? Besides, I do not understand your doctrine, though I must give up my own. Sometimes you preach up Moses stoutly, and then suddenly Jesus Christ is all in all. One while you talk notably of being born again, and then presently you seem to speak as if my own obedience was fit only to destroy me. Pray explain yourself, and do not leave me in the dark. You have blown my candle out, and in civility should lend me your lanthorn.

Nay, sir, candle-light will not serve you here. Sun-light is wanted; rays from the sun of righteousness, or you continue dark, notwithstanding all that I can say. May this light be granted.

The law is preached for two reasons, first as a *school-master to bring men unto Christ, that they may be justified by faith;* and, secondly, as a *rule of life* to walk with Christ, but as no condition of salvation.

Jesus Christ has no business with a Pharisee, who can plead his own righteousness. He came to *seek and to save them that are lost.* And the moral law must be preached in its utmost rigor, to awaken every sort of sinners, and convince them of their *lost* estate. When the law is set home by the Holy Spirit, it becomes a school-master, sharp indeed, and scourges sinners unto Christ. The fox is then unkennelled, and driven from his old haunt, sincere obedience, the common refuge and convenient screen for drunkards, fornicators, liars, thieves, and simpering deists, who are all at their wits' end presently, when they find their thatched hovel in a blaze.

No sooner is the rigor of the law perceived by the

understanding, and felt in the conscience, but it forces every one to say, as Paul did, *When the commandment came*, came home to my heart, *I died*, all hope of life through my own obedience perished. And they can take up Paul's lamentation, a mighty strange one to a modern Christian who has got no feeling, *O wretched man that I am! who shall deliver me from this body of death?*

Now they know, by good experience, that *death is the wages of sin;* and feel themselves in a state of condemnation. This makes them dread sin, and free to part with it; because it has lost its painted cheek, and shews its haggard countenance. The prayers of the church become very suitable and welcome. The frequent supplication of "Lord, have mercy on us," is neither loathsome nor tiresome. The much repeated cry "for mercy on us miserable sinners," is not thought a cry too much. And those strong communion words, "the remembrance of our sins is grievous and the burden of them is intolerable," are not muttered by hollow lip, but uttered with a feeling heart.

A sinner, thus convinced of sin, struggles hard to help himself. He watches, strives and prays, and fain would keep the whole law. But as he strives, the law opens to his view, and shows its spiritual nature, and its marvellous extent; reaching to every action, word, and thought, and calling for obedience every moment. And now he feels his nature's sad depravity. His heart is earthly and unclean, and therefore has a fixed dislike to spiritual duties. It may be *forced* on them, but cannot *relish* them, nor keep a *full attention* to them. He could sit four hours in an idle playhouse; and though crowded up exceedingly, could keep a fixed attention all the time, and be sorry when the farce was over. But his heart goes to prayer, like an idle boy to school, sauntering every step, and would play truant, if he dare.

After many fruitless struggles to keep the law, he finds himself *without strength.* Fain he would delight in God, and in his spiritual service, but he cannot. His nature will not kindly move towards God, and when thrust upon the task, groweth quarrelsome or sleepy, and is quickly jaded down. Hence he finds an utter need of the Spirit's aid, to create his heart anew, and breathe some *spiritual life*, to enable him for *spiritual service.*

The *curse* of the law has now made known his *guilt ;* the *spirituality* of the law has shewn his *depraved nature ;* and his *vain attempts* to keep the law have disclosed his *utter feebleness.* Thus the law has prepared him for Christ. His heart is humbled, and broken down with an awful sense of his guiltiness and filthiness and feebleness. He is possessed of the first beatitude, *Poverty of spirit,* but does not yet know it is the leading step unto the kingdom of heaven.

This first beatitude conducts him to the second, *Blessed are the mourners.* He mourns, because he is poor in spirit, sensible of his spirit's poverty ; stripped of all his fancied worth, and fancied ability to help himself; *weary* of sin and of his evil heart ; *heavy-laden* with a guilty burden, and seeking rest but finding none.

Pray, doctor, who is this sorry fellow, this weary wretch, that comes to Jesus Christ with such a loaded pack upon his back ? Some highwayman, no doubt, or some housebreaker ; perhaps a murderer ; at least a person excommunicate, who has been very naughty

Indeed, sir, this sorry fellow is the doctor himself, and every one who comes aright to Jesus Christ. Did you never read the invitation which he makes to sinners? *Come unto me, all ye that labor and are heavy laden, and I will give you rest.* You are a sinner, sir; and all men are sinners, and condemned by the law; but all men do not feel their condemnation, and therefore are not heavy laden with a guilty burden, or laboring after rest. Yet only such are invited, and only such are accepted. What right have you to come to Jesus Christ, unless you come in his appointed way?

If your wealthy neighbor should invite his poor parish widows to dine on Sundays at his house, this invitation would give you no right to dine, nor yet the vicar. You are not *poor widows*. And supposing you should borrow female clothing, put on a gown and petticoat, and call yourself a *poor widow*, this female dress would not procure a right to dine, but might expose you to a cudgel. Yet this is now become the genteel way of coming unto Jesus. Men borrow at a church the garb and language of a Christian, and say most sad things of themselves, while they are upon their knees, as if they were *poor sinners* truly, and yet would execrate a preacher, who should say the same things in a pulpit, which they had uttered in a pew.

You have heard, no doubt, of beggars who tie a leg up when they go a begging, and then make hideous lamentation of their lameness. Why, this is just your case, sir. When you go to church a praying, which is begging, you tie your righteous heart up, and then make woful outcry for *mercy on us miserable sinners.* Oh, sir, these tricks may pass a while unnoticed; but Jesus Christ will apprehend such cheats at last, and give them their desert.

Would you know where God will cast a gracious eye? He tells you, *To this man will I look, saith the Lord, even to him that is poor and contrite*, poor in spirit, and bruised with a sense of his sinfulness.

And would you hear whom Jesus calls? His own lips inform you, *I am not come to call the righteous.* No; why should he? If he did, they would not come in his way, for they have found a better. But I am come, he saith, *to call sinners* — sinners sensible of sin, and bruised with it; and to call them daily *to repentance* — not to patter over good confessions with a frozen lip, but to breathe them from a mourning heart. St. Luke introduces the call with these words, *The whole need no physician, but the sick.* And pray, sir, who are the *whole?* Have any kept the *whole* law without offending in a single point? Not a man. Then all are condemned by the law, and have passed under its curse. Yet many think themselves *whole*, or *nearly* whole, and therefore see *no need*, or *little need* of Christ's atonement. Alas for such! when the stone they have rejected falls upon them, it will grind them unto powder. But the *sick* need a physician. They feel that woful sickness, the *plague of the heart*, and loathe themselves in dust and ashes.

But we must take a little further notice of our young pilgrim, before we drop him altogether. He was left disconsolate, with raw back and weeping eyes, just flogged out of Moses' school, and seeking balm to heal his wounds, but finding none. At length the invitation of Jesus reaches his ears, *Come unto me, thou heavy laden soul, and I will give thee rest.* He hears and wonders, listens and is pleased. A gleam of joy steals in his heart — a joy he never felt before, springing from a cheering hope and dawning prospect of deliverance. This kindles high esteem and kind affection for the Saviour, who appears all lovely in his sight, and often draws a heavenly tear from his eyes. The name of Jesus groweth musical, his love adorable, and his salvation above all things desirable.

The weeping sinner enters now upon a new world, and joins himself with the praying citizens of Sion. Jesus is welcomed as his King and Saviour, and receives hosannahs from him. He begins to understand what grace means, even mercy, rich mercy freely shewn to a lost and ruined sinner. No sermon suits him now but what directs his heart to Jesus, and sets the Saviour forth as prophet, priest, and king to save his people. A full and free salvation captivates his heart. 'Tis just the thing he wants, and therefore highly welcome. And whilst the tidings of this royal grace are sounding in his ears, he seems to give them credit; but when the book is laid aside, or sermon over, fresh doubts arise which much perplex him. His understanding is enlightened, but his heart retains a *legal bias*, and a secret harping after merit still. Sometimes he fears the Gospel tidings are so good, they are not true; or if they may be true, they are too good for him. He likes and wants the promised grace, but *staggers* at the promise, A sense of guilt and his uncleanness so dismay him, that he dares not bring a filthy naked soul to Jesus, to be washed and clothed by him.

Sincere obedience often peeps again, and bids the pilgrim wash himself first, and Jesus Christ shall *rinse* him afterwards; bids him plant a fig leaf here and there, and make a patched frock of duty; and if it prove too scanty, Jesus shall eke it out with his fine linen. This expedient pleases for a season, and to work he goes, hoping to make himself so fair and tight, that Jesus Christ shall fall in love with him, and give him *rare commendation* instead of *free pardon*. But *though he wash himself in snow-water, and make his hands exceeding clean, he is plunged in the ditch again, and his own clothes abhor him.* Thus he grows bewildered, and has lost the sight of grace, until he hears it preached afresh; and then he drops the snow-water and hastens to the *fountain opened for sin and for uncleanness.* He stands upon the brink, but cannot enter; and longeth a washing, but must wait for the moving of the water. He views the fountain, and sees it *fair* and *open;* he views the promise and sees it *full* and *clear — He that believeth shall be saved;* which makes him cry, "Oh, that I could believe the promise; Jesus then would save me. But my heart staggers, and, when my foot seems fixed upon the rock, a sudden gust of doubts blows me in the mire again."

Now he knows the meaning of St. Paul's words, *Believe in Jesus Christ, and thou shalt be saved;* and he clearly understands that his want of pardon, peace, and holiness, is owing to his want of faith. If he could believe, Jesus Christ would fulfil his promise—it would be *done according to his faith.* Jesus Christ would save him from the *guilt* and *power* of sin.

This makes him feel his want of faith, and his want of

power to give it. He had been nursed in a Christian land, and thought a mere assent to Scripture was sufficient ground to make him a believer; and he marvelled that some preachers made a mighty stir about this easy matter. But he finds this human faith will neither purify his heart, nor wash his conscience: it will not save from sin. And he feels that prayer is nothing, and procureth nothing, without divine faith. He sees a reason why the chosen twelve should say, *Lord, increase our faith,* because it is the gift of God. Could they give themselves one grain, they might add another, yea, a dozen grains, or twenty; and had no need to ask for that they could give themselves. Besides, these men who ask for faith, were not heathen men, but Christian men, true followers of Christ; and none but such can pray for faith with a hearty feeling of their want of it.

Doctor, you talk mightily of unbelievers. Pray, where may they grow? In Lapland, among the witches; or in Greenland, among the whale-fishers? Sure the people of England are staunch believers, and very good Christians. A modern set, I own, is started up among us, who think it courage to defy their Maker, and *act as freely* as if they could control him; and if they *think as freely* as they act, may well be called *free thinkers.* Such people cannot value Jesus Christ, because he brings hell-tidings to their ears. Who can love a messenger of ill news? Mahomet would prove a sweeter prophet for this light-heeled gentry; and would gain much credit, could he gain the pulpit, for he allows men concubines enough. However, these are but a few rotten pears among the heap; the rest are sound; and I can vouchsafe for our own parish, they are all believers. Indeed, doctor, it would do you good to see how smirkingly they go to church in summer; and how tidily they look at church, with their better coats and gowns on.

Oh, sir, the lifeless manner in which people pray, or hear the word of God at church, sheweth plainly that they have no property in the blessings of the Gospel. Glorious things are spoken in the Scripture, but they make a mighty small impression on a Christian congregation. The heavenly tidings fall into their heavy ears like money dropt into a dead man's hand. No comfort is received from the money or the tidings, because they are both dead, and have no interest in them.

If you, sir, was an heir to a fine estate, your bosom would be often warmed with the joyful prospect; but your father's servant could not feel your joy. His bosom would not glow when the fields are viewed, or when the rents are paid. And wherefore? Because he is not the heir.

A Bible is the precious store-house, and the magna charta of a Christian. There he reads of his heavenly Father's love, and of his dying Saviour's legacies. There he sees a map of his travels through the wilderness, and a landscape too of Canaan. And when he climbs on Pisgah's top, and views the promised land, his heart begins to burn, delighted with the blessed prospect, and amazed at the rich and free salvation. But a mere professor, though a decent one, looks on the Bible as a dull book; and peruseth it with such indifference as you would read the title-deeds belonging to another man's estate.

I am quite amazed to hear you vouch for your parish as a whole flock of believers. Such a thing was never known before, and would make an eighth wonder of the world. Why, sir, are there none among you that are slaves to divers lusts and pleasures? None that live in malice and envy, hateful and hating one another? Have you no drunkards nor whoremongers, no Sabbath-breakers nor common swearers, no extortioners nor covetous, no liars nor thieves, no lazy hands that will not work, and no light minds that cannot pray? If you think such church-goers are believers, I may fairly rank Satan at their head; because he stands possessed of their faith, and is the noble captain of this troop — a troop which often maketh up three quarters of a parish.

Jesus says, *He that believeth shall be saved.* Saved from what? Why, from the *guilt* and *power* of sin. Such is Christ's salvation here on earth. But this black troop is visibly and wilfully under the power of sin, and therefore cannot have that faith which saves from sin.

Thus at once reckoning, the greater part of your sheep prove goats or wolves; but a remnant is behind of *decent* people, the modern soft phrase for a Christian. Let these decent people take a decent trial. It will not hurt them, if they are good men and true.

St. Paul says, *Examine yourselves, whether ye be in the faith.* He takes it not for granted that Christian professors must be true believers, but commands them all to *prove their own selves;* and drops a question, as a touchstone, to prove themselves by. A strange question it must seem to such as have not true faith, yet is a most important question, and the only one that distinguisheth true faith from counterfeit. The apostle does not ask, whether you are sober, honest, charitable, church-going people — the present pigmy standard for a Christian soldier — but he asks a very searching question, even this, *Know ye not that Jesus Christ is* in *you?* And declares, if they know it not, they must be *reprobates*, disapproved of God as hypocrites, notwithstanding all their decent carriage.

The meaning of St. Paul's question is plainly this, *Know ye not that* the Spirit of *Christ is in you?* For where Christ's Spirit is, there is he. The same kind of question is asked in the first epistle, *Know ye not, that ye are the temple of God, and that the Spirit of God dwelleth in you.*

Very right, doctor, here we are agreed. All Christians, to be sure, must have the Spirit of Christ; and though we feel it not, but are utter strangers to its influence, we must be supposed to have it; because we are born in a Christian land, wear a Christian name, breathe a wholesome Christian air, have a pew in a Christian church, keep a merry Christmas every year, and bury upon Christian ground. Here is proof enough, doctor.

Yes, sir, proof enough that you live in a Christian land, but no proof that you are a Christian people. To suppose you have the Spirit's presence, and yet remain an utter stranger to its influence, is the topmost tower of enthusiasm, the soaring pinnacle on which its floating weathercock is fixed. So this blessed guest comes to lurk in your bosom, like a spy in a camp; or like a thief in a cellar; and stealeth in and stealeth out, without your notice: mighty fine! But you are not such a wild enthusiast in common life as to suppose their is money in your pocket, when you feel none; or bank notes in your drawer, when you find none. If you never feel any symptoms of patience, you cannot well suppose yourself possessed of any; and why should you dream of the Spirit's presence, when you never find any tokens of it?

The Spirit's influence must be felt, or it cannot profit; and the very offices of the Holy Spirit do suppose and warrant such a *feeling*. Let me mention some of them, which are these — *to quicken; to strengthen mightily; to witness our adoption* and *to bring heavenly joy*. Now sir, what avails that *quickening*, which I cannot feel? It leaves me just as heartless to spiritual duty as it found me. And what advantage does that *mighty strengthening* bring, which is not perceived by me? It yields no further power to subdue my lusts than I had before. And of what service is that *witness* in the court of conscience who speaks in such a low or mumbling tone, that none can hear or understand him? I am just as well without his evidence as with it. And lastly, of what use or value is that *heavenly joy*, which I can have no taste of? All this is just the picture of Isaiah's hungry man who *dreamt he was eating, but awoke and was empty*.

But, sir, St. Paul did not ask this idle question, "Do you *suppose* the Spirit of Christ is in you?" All the Church of Corinth, and all the churchmen in Great Britain, might have answered quickly, "Yes, Mr. Paul, we do *suppose* it." But he asks a weighty question, "Do ye *know* it?" Have you real experience, or heartfelt knowledge, that the Spirit of Christ is in you? Are you acquainted with its operation? Do you *know* it?

St. Paul may ask this question safely, because his name is canonized, and his bones are mouldered into dust; but if a living preacher ask the same question, the world cry out, enthusiasm! And yet St. Paul makes this very *knowledge* the very evidence of true faith; and accounteth other faith, which produceth not this knowledge, to be counterfeit; and the men themselves to be reprobates.

Jesus saith to his disciples, *Ye know the Spirit, for he dwelleth with you.* His words carry this plain meaning, that where the Spirit dwells, he makes his presence *known* by his operations on the heart.

St. John tells the whole Christian Church, *Hereby we know that Christ dwelleth in us, by his Spirit, which he hath given us.* We *know* the Spirit of Christ dwelleth in us, and thereby are assured of our union with Christ. And, like as Paul had done before, he proposeth this knowledge as a touchstone, to try our profession — *hereby* we know that Christ dwelleth in us.

Indeed, doctor, I am a stranger to the Holy Spirit's influence, yet do not seem disposed to question my profession. Still, I think my faith is sound, and am sure there is no better in the parish. The vicar never questioned it; and why should you? It is not mighty civil. Besides, I am free of my beer, and have the good luck to be loved by every one — scarce a dog will bark at me. 'As honest as the old grazier,' is a common saying; and this alone is proof enough that I must be a Christian.

Indeed, sir, this alone is proof enough against your Christianity. *While you are of the world, the world will love you; but when you cease to be of the world, and are chosen out of the world, the world will hate you.* It hated Jesus Christ, and will hate every true disciple.

Paul affirms peremptorily, *Yea, and all that will live godly in Christ Jesus shall suffer persecution.* Live *where* you will, in a Christian or a heathen land; live *when* you will, in the present or distant age, Paul affirms universally of real Christians, *Yea, they* all *shall suffer persecution.* If you lead what the world calls a godly life, you will have the world's condemnation. You may be sober, and honest, and friendly; you may pray, and give alms, and fast too, if you please; and, while these things are doing by your own strength, and make a ground of acceptance with God, you are waxing godly *in yourself*, or from yourself made godly by the world's spirit, and the world will applaud you. But, if once you grow godly in *Christ Jesus*, renouncing all your wisdom, strength, and righteousness, and come to Jesus as a lost sinner, seeking all supplies from him, resting all your hope upon him, making him your all in every thing, and counting all things utter dross in comparison of him, then the world will hate you, and lift a heel against you. A godly life *in Christ Jesus* thwarteth human pride, and staineth all its glory, which will not be suffered patiently.

Men are mighty apt to bless themselves in the world's esteem, and look upon it as a kindly token that the Lord accepts them. To rectify the judgment, and sweep away deceitful hopes, arising from the world's good name, Christ has dropt a *curse* upon it, saying, *Woe unto you, when all men shall speak well of you.* This is one of the Lord's *Shibboleths*, which he useth to alarm a decent professor, the world's favorite. It is a frightful ugly bridge upon the king's highway. An Israelite goes over safely, but no Edomite can pass it. Esau, the elder brother will not travel here, but trudgeth down to a ferry, built by Mr. *Fairspeech*, to make a smoother passage over the river.

So much for the world's esteem: happy is the man who has lost it wholly and honestly. But your faith, sir, must be canvassed a little more. You are a grazier, it seems; and when you buy a bullock at a fair, you do not take the salesman's word, but feel the beast yourself, and examine all its points minutely. Now, sir, do the same by your faith, and take it not on trust, as recommended by your neighbor, but examine it, and handle all its points by the word of God. Faith is an active and a fruitful thing, its fruit is pleasant both to God and man. And the man who does possess it, is a noble man indeed — an heir of God through Christ. But it behoves us to be wary, for counterfeit faith, like counterfeit gold, is very current.

Paul says, *Being justified by faith we have peace with God, through our Lord Jesus Christ;* we *have* peace, or *possess* it, for what we *have* we must possess. Now, this peace is given to assure the conscience that God is at peace with us — that he is reconciled, and has forgiven all our trespasses. And whoever feels this peace must be assured of the pardon of his sins; it is the witness of his pardon.

This blessed peace does not grow in nature's garden, nor can be digged out of mines of human merit. It was lost in Paradise, and is found *only* at Calvary. It is called the peace of God because it is of God's bestowing, and bestowed through Jesus Christ *alone*.

Where this peace is bestowed, it is found to be as Paul describes it, A *peace passing all understanding.* A peace so exquisitely rich that none can understand what it is until he feels it; and when he feels it never can express it. Men may mistake this peace before they taste it, as ten thousands do, and take up with a *human calm*, instead of it; but he who feels it never can mistake it, for nothing else is like it — it passeth all understanding.

The Holy Spirit seals this peace upon the conscience, and thereby proclaims the pardon of sin, and *sheds abroad the love of God into the heart*, and *beareth witness to our adoption.*

This sealing of the Holy Spirit is given as an *earnest of our future inheritance*; it is a heavenly pledge dropt into the bosom to assure us of our interest in Christ. Thus conscience is delivered from the fear of wrath, and *fear of death which bringeth bondage;* the heart rejoices now in God, as a reconciled God, calls him *Father by the Spirit of adoption*, delighteth in his blessed service, and feels the meaning of St. Peter's words, *Believing in Christ Jesus, ye rejoice with joy* unspeakable, *and full of* GLORY.

These are weighty words, directed unto all believing churches, and experienced by them; but never were, and never will be felt by a mere human faith, springing from the human intellect. The faith producing heavenly peace, and the peace produced, are both the gift of God.

By the help of this divine faith, the happy Christian now repeats his church hymns with truth and pleasure: "My soul doth magnify the Lord, and my spirit hath *rejoiced* in God my Saviour." Or with old Simeon, "Let thy servant depart in peace, O Lord, for mine eyes have *seen* thy salvation."

Now, sir, hear what your own peace is. You feel no distress of mind, but are mighty easy, and your calm, which is a *dead calm*, ariseth from your character, though a sinful character at best. Your peace brings no heavenly joy, and so comes not from heaven, neither does it flow *entirely* through the golden conduit of the Saviour's merit, but drippeth from a rotten wooden pipe of your own duties. You are, it seems, a cheerful, harmless creature, like a robin-red-breast, who is much respected everywhere; and you frequent the church, as many a pious mouse will, yet does not like her quarters: prayer-books are dry champing — a pantry suits her better. And you see many who are worse than yourself, abundantly, which makes you hope your state is good; and, while outward things go smooth, your *calm* continues. But when calamities come on, and thicken as they come, your peace is gone; it cannot stand a tempest. And when your soul is hovering on a sick bed for its flight, it will either feel a *dead security*, or take a *frightful leap* into another world. Unless you are supported by divine faith, you cannot sing the Christian's dying song, *O death, where is thy sting? O grave, where is thy victory?*

Now, sir, we proceed to another point of faith, and a choice one too, very savory and nourishing to a true believer. St. Peter tells us that *faith purifies the heart;* and St. John affirms, *This is the victory whereby we overcome the world, even our faith;* and he tells us what he means by the world, even *the lust of the flesh, the lust of the eye, and the pride of life.*

Come, sir, bring your face to the gospel-glass, and handle this point well, like an old grazier. Does your faith overcome the *lust of the flesh*, making you victorious over your palate, and over outward pollution, and inward uncleanness?

Does your faith overcome the *lust of the eye*, and keep your heart from gasping after more wealth, more preferment, or more honors? *Having food and raiment, have you learnt therewith to be content?*

Does your faith overcome the *pride of life*, and prevent your being charmed with a lofty house, rich furniture, genteel equipage, and splendid raiment? Does it make you sick of earthly vanities, and draw your heart to things above?

Speak, sir, and speak honestly. If you are a slave to these matters, and a quiet slave, you may keep your faith, Satan will not steal it from you. The devils do *believe*, and tremble, but are devils still.

One point more, sir, and we have done. Faith is not only intended to *pacify* the conscience, and *purify* the heart, but also to *rescue* the mind from earthly troubles. Our passage through life is attended with storms. We sail upon a boisterous sea, where many tempests are felt, and many are feared which look black and bode mischief, but pass over. Now faith is designed for an anchor to keep the mind steady, and give it rest; even as Isaiah saith, *Thou wilt keep him in perfect peace, whose mind is stayed on thee, because he trusteth in thee.*

Precious promises, suited to our wants, are scattered through the Bible, and divine faith will feed upon the promises, looking unto Jesus to fulfil them, but human faith can reap no profit from them. Let me suppose you in distressful circumstances, and, while musing on them with an anxious heart, you cast a look upon a distant Bible. The book is fetched and opened, and this passage meets your eye, *Call upon me in the day of trouble, I will deliver thee, and thou shalt glorify me.* Here you view a gracious promise, made by a faithful God, and made without limitation or condition, directed unto every one that reads or hears it, applicable to every time of trouble, and requiring *only* prayer of faith for deliverance. Yet, sir, it is possible this blessed promise might not even draw a prayer from you: perhaps it gains a little musing, and the book is closed; or, if it should extort a feeble cry, the prayer does not ease your heart, nor fetch deliverance, for want of faith.

You know the word of Jesus, *all things whatsoever ye shall ask in prayer*, believing, *ye shall receive.* But for want of faith, your reasoning heart will ask, "From whence can this deliverance come?" What is that to you, sir? God keeps the means of deliverance out of sight, on purpose to exercise our faith, but promises to *make a way for our escape*, though we can see none.

Or perhaps you may surmise, "This promise, was not meant for me; I am not worthy of it." Sir, God's promise is not made to compliment your worthiness, but to manifest the riches of his grace in Christ Jesus. Did you mind how the promise runs? It is not said, "Glorify me *first* and afterward "I will deliver thee," which would be making man's worthiness a foundation for God's blessing; but he says, "I will deliver thee, and then thou shalt glorify me."

Faith considers all the promises as freely made to supply our wants, and rest upon the Lord's faithfulness to fulfil them; and when a promise is fulfilled, adores the mercy, and glorifies the Lord for it. In this way, and this only, he gets some hearty rent of praise. Such free deliverance wins the heart, and binds it to the Lord, and makes obedience cheerful.

I know a man who spends his income yearly, because he has no family; as little as he can upon himself, and the rest upon his neighbors. He keeps no purse against a rainy day, and wants none: Jesus Christ is his banker, and a very able one. Sometimes, by sickness, or unforeseen expenses, he gets behind hand—and greatly so. At such times, he does not run about among his earthly friends to seek relief, but falleth on his knees, and calls upon his banker, saying, "Lord, I am in want, and thou must help me. Here I bring thy gracious promise, look upon it, Jesus. It says, *Call upon me in the time of trouble, I will deliver thee, and thou shalt glorify me.* Lord, I call, and thou dost hear; I believe, and thou art faithful; be it now unto me according to thy word." Such prayers, he said, never failed to bring supplies—some from those who cared for him, and some from such as did avoid his company. For Jesus Christ has every heart and purse in his own hand, and often makes a raven feed his prophets, or makes the *earth to help the woman*, to shew his finger clearly in such deliverance.

Scripture promises are real bank-notes of heaven, and the true riches of believers, who do not live on stock in hand, but traffic with this paper currency. Where divine faith is found, it takes the notes to Christ's bank and receives the cash. But human faith cannot traffic with this paper, it reads the notes, and owns them good, but dares not take them to the skies for payment. No faith can truly act on God but that which comes from God.

Prayer of faith, exercised with perseverance, surely brings deliverance, if not immediately, yet at a proper season; and, till deliverance comes, the *mind is stayed on God, and kept in perfect peace.* Faith picks the thorns out of the flesh, and takes the rankling pain away before the wound is healed.

Truly, doctor, now you make me thoughtful. My faith will not produce the precious fruit you have mentioned. It brings no peace passing all understanding, affords no real victory over the world, and yields no sweet relief in time of trouble. It picks no thorns out of my flesh: it must be counterfeit. My support in trouble arises from my purse, or from my friends, and not from faith. Yet I cannot comprehend how a mere reliance on God's promise can charm away our grief, and set the heart at rest before deliverance comes. This seems a charm indeed!

So it is, sir, and a most delightful charm; yet not fanciful, but real, having good foundation in our nature. Where divine faith is given, it will act on God as human faith will act on man, and produce the same effects. A case will make my meaning plan.

I suppose you, as before, fallen in great distress, and a lawyer's letter is received, bringing doleful tidings that your person will be seized unless your debts are paid within a month. While the letter is perusing, an old acquaintance calls upon you, sees a gloom upon your face, and ask the cause of it. You put the letter in his hand: he reads, and drops a friendly tear. After some little pause he says, "Old friend, I have not the cash at present by me, but engage to pay your debts before the month is out." Now, sir, if you thought this person was not *able* to discharge your debts, or not to be *relied* on, because his mind was fickle, his promise would bring no relief, because it gains no credit. You have no faith in him. But if you knew the man was able, and might be trusted, his promise would relieve you instantly. A firm reliance on his word would take away your burden, and set your mind at ease, before the debt was paid.

Well, sir, if a firm reliance on the word of man has this sweet influence on the heart, a firm reliance on the word of God will have the same. Why should it not? God's word deserveth as much credit, surely, as the word of man. He is as able to perform, and as faithful to fulfil his promise as your neighbor. *No one ever trusted in him and was confounded.* And where the *mind is stayed on God, it will be kept in perfect peace,* before deliverance comes. Such may say, with David, *God is our refuge, therefore we will not fear, though the earth be removed, and the mountains carried into the midst of the sea.* Or with Habakkuk, *Though the fig-tree should not blossom, nor fruit be in the vine; though the olive too should fail, and the fields yield no meat; though the flock be cut off from the fold, and no herd be found in the stalls, yet will I rejoice in the Lord; I will joy in the God of my salvation.* The prop of God's faithful word cannot break; and a human heart, resting firmly on it, never can sink; and men might learn to feel their unbelief, for want of this support in trouble. The prop stands ready on the king's highroad, to support all weary passengers, but they have not faith to lean upon it, else they would find rest.

In speculation, it seems as easy to trust a faithful God as trust and upright man; but in practice it is found otherwise. When trials come, men cannot trust a faithful God without divine assistance — so trust him as to cast their burden on him, and obtain his perfect peace. Here the charm of faith ceaseth, because there is no faith to charm.

If, in time of trouble, some prospect of deliverance is afforded by a human arm, men often put a cheat upon themselves, and talk of trusting God, while they are only leaning on a human shoulder. Remove this earthly prop, and take away all human prospect of relief, and the man cries out, "What must I do? I am undone." He cannot rest upon God's *naked* word, nor seat his heart upon the solid chair of promise, without some human stool beside.

Faith is just the same thing now it was in Abraham's day *who, against hope, believed in hope.* He had no human prospect of an heir, and yet expected one, relying wholly on God's *naked* promise. And a *naked* promise is the *whole* support of divine faith now. Jesus Christ will admit no partner for our faith. He is worthy of *full* credit, and expects it; and we must either look to him *alone*, or look to be confounded. He will be all or nothing.

Nay, doctor, now you press too hard upon Jesus Christ. He is a very good Saviour, to be sure, but we must not put upon him neither. What? lay all the burden of salvation on him! This does not seem reasonable, nor is it using him handsomely. So he must do all the work, and I must stand by as a lazy thief, to see it done. No, no, doctor, I shall not make a packhorse of my Saviour, but would use him with good manners; and, whilst I look for great things from him, will try to do something for myself.

Sir, the best manners you can shew towards superiors

is to do as you are bid, and not gainsay their orders, by a wilful pertness, or an ill-timed modesty. You honor Jesus by employing him as a *whole* Saviour, and you rob him of his glory, and excite his indignation, when you steal a portion of his royal sceptre, or his priestly censer, or his prophet's staff from him. He is appointed for a Saviour—not a scanty, but a full one — and he never does his work by halves. The work creates no hurry, and is found no burden. He speaks, or wills, and it is done. Do not, therefore, compliment him with your idle manners, but obey his orders, which are these, *Look unto me and be saved, all the ends of the earth, for I am God and none else,* or nothing less, and therefore able to save. Jesus does not beg of you to look a little to yourself, and the rest to him ; but commands you to look singly unto him for heavenly wisdom to direct you, for heavenly peace to bless you, and for heavenly grace to sanctify you. And he has left a faithful word for your encouragement, that *whosoever believeth* (or trusteth) *in him, shall be saved* —saved from spiritual darkness, and from the guilt and power of sin.

You talk of looking to yourself, which bespeaks some confidence in yourself, but Jesus has pronounced a curse on every *human* confidence. Hear his awful declaration, *Thus saith the Lord, cursed is the man who trusteth in man,* (in himself or in another), *he shall be like the heath in the desert, and shall not see when good cometh.* But take the blessing too, and may it reach your heart. *Blessed is the man who trusteth in the Lord, and whose hope the Lord is ; he shall be like a tree planted by the waters, which spreadeth out its roots by the river, and does not regard when drought cometh, but its leaf is green, and it never ceaseth yielding fruit.*

If your eye is *single*, directed *wholly* unto Christ, you will be full of light and peace; but if your eye is *double*, peeping upon Jesus, and squinting towards men, you will be full of darkness, and be at length confounded.

The life of faith is called *the fight of faith;* and truly called so. For, where divine faith is given, it is seldom exercised without a conflict in the heart, which loves an earthly refuge, and dreads a *naked* promise; dearly loves a human prop, and always seeks some wooden buttress to support God's iron pillar.

On this account, men dare not singly trust in Christ's *atonement* for their peace, but clap their feeble shoulder to his cross, to strengthen it; nor dare they rest on Jesus' *grace*, to make them holy, but call up human arms to stay gigantic lusts within; nor can they trust in Jesus' *guidance* to make them wise unto salvation, but call the wisdom of the world in, an utter night-piece, to chase away the world's darkness.

Many yet are so obliging as to let the Saviour have a share in the work of man's salvation, but Jesus does not thank them for this condescension. He rejects that faith which does not centre in him *only*, and rest the heart *entirely* on him. He wants no partner, and will admit of none; nor were he worthy of the name of Saviour, if salvation was not *wholly* from him.

Hear what he says of himself, *I have trodden the winepress* alone: *I looked and there was* none *to help; therefore mine* own *arm brought salvation.*

Hear what a prophet says of him, *Behold! the* Lord

God *will come with a strong hand, and* his *arm shall rule:* he *shall feed his flock like a shepherd,* he *shall gather the lambs with* his *arm, and he shall carry them in his bosom.* Where, you may observe, all partners are excluded from this work. The Lord Jesus, who is called the *Lord God,* shall act the part of a shepherd, and lay down his life for the sheep; and, by treading the winepress *alone,* shall make the atonement *himself:* then he will *gather* the flock, and *feed* the flock, and *carry* the flock home *himself.* Jesus Christ does not help you to help yourself; but he does the whole work himself: *his* own *arm shall rule.*

Indeed, where men are quickened by the Holy Spirit, and well convinced of their sinfulness and helplessness, they are now enabled to use the means of grace properly, and must use them diligently, but the *whole work* still is in the Saviour's hand. He must guide the understanding, by his Spirit, into all saving truth; he must bring his blood-bought peace to the conscience; he must tame the tempers, sanctify the affections, and make us cheerfully disposed for all good works. Our business is to watch and pray, and it is the Saviour's office to *work in us to will and do.* What will and power he gives, we may exercise, and nothing more. He only can increase it who first gave it.

Paul says, *It has pleased the Father, that in Christ Jesus,* (in his human nature, as a temple), *all fulness should dwell. All fulness* of wisdom to direct us, of power to protect us, of grace to pardon and sanctify us. And this *all fulness* is treasured up in Christ the head, to be communicated to the members of his body. Whatever wisdom, strength, peace, or righteousness are not received from this storehouse, by faith, are spurious, a mere tinsel ware, which may glitter much, but has no value.

Paul says further, *Christ is all and in all.* He is possessed of an *all fulness*, that he might be not *something* only in our wisdom, strength, peace, and righteousness, but *all* in every thing, and *all* in every person; *all* in the Greek as well as the barbarian; *all* in the scholar as well as in the rustic.

And St. John says, *We beheld Christ's glory, full of grace and truth; and out of his fulness have we all received, even grace for grace.* Where the apostle shews that a believer's business is to receive supplies of grace out of Christ's fulness.

Doctor, I cannot comprehend that Jesus Christ must be all in *wisdom* to a scholar, as well as to a countryman. If human learning will not help to make us wise unto salvation, of what use is it, and wherefore do we value it? My landlord is reckoned a monstrous scholar: he has been at Cambridge, and travelled abroad, and talks French at a wonderful rate. He is always at his books; and makes eclipses when he pleaseth. We hear he put in four into Dyer's almanac the last year. One day he took me into his study, and showed me all his learning. Bless me, what a sight! More books, by half, upon his shelves, than I have bullocks in my pastures! And they seem well handled, for I did not spy a mouldy book in the study, except an old Bible, which lay drooping in a corner. I suppose it was his grandfather's. Now, doctor, does it not seem likely that my landlord must get more Christian knowledge from his vast gilded heap of books than I can get from a plain single Bible?

Human science, sir, keeps men out of mischief, trains them up for civil occupations, and oft produceth notable discoveries, which are useful to the world; but never can lead the heart to Jesus Christ, nor breed a single grain of faith in him. They who know most of *human* science, and have waded deepest in it, know the most of its vanities, and find it but vexation of spirit.

The heavenly oracles declare *the wisdom of the world is foolishness with God;* and tell us, *not many wise are called* to possess the gospel kingdom. And surely God would never brand the wisdom of the world as folly, if it had the least tendency to make men wise unto salvation.

It will, I think, be found a certain truth, that when human science is cultivated eagerly in a Christian country, the study of the Bible always grows neglected; and that immorality and infidelity spread their branches equally with human science; and that a learned nation, when arrived to its highest pitch of human science, is just become ripe for slavery, and doomed to *perpetual* bondage. Witness Egypt, Greece, and Rome.

Bible knowledge, fetched in by prayer, and watered well with meditation, makes the mind humble and serious; but human science lifts men up, makes them *vain in their imagination, darkens the foolish heart* still more, and thereby drives them farther off from God. The present age is no bad comment on the following Scripture: *The world by wisdom knew not God.*

Solomon gave his heart to seek wisdom, and knew more of the secrets of nature than any man; yet he found no real profit from his study, but calls it *vanity, and a sore travail which the sons of men are exercised with.* This is left on holy record, to direct us what to think of human science; and they who laugh at the direction may chance to weep at last, as Grotius did, and repeat his dying lamentation.

Pray, doctor, what was it?

Why, sir, as he lay lamenting on his death-bed, calling himself the *poor publican*, mentioned in the parable, and wishing he might change conditions with *John Urick*, a poor but devout man, some that were present spake to Grotius of his great industry and learned performances, and spake of them with admiration; to which he replied. with a sigh, " Heu! vitam perdidi operose nihil agendo;" Alas! I have squandered my life away laboriously in doing nothing.

The learned Selden also, his antagonist, was very much of his mind, when he came to die.

Sir, if you would learn wisdom in the school of Christ, Paul affirms, *You must become a fool, in order to be wise.* A crabbed lesson truly, to be learned by a scholar! and a mighty strange expression, yet exceeding proper for a scribe, to wake him from his fond delirium, and fetch him to his senses. He needs such amazing language to make him pause, and gaze about for a meaning. It is a block thrown in his way, to stop his vain pursuit. It tells a scholar he must go empty unto Jesus, and see himself a fool in heavenly science; as much in daily want of a teacher here, as an idiot is of some director in his worldly business.

The master of the school speaks the same kind of language to his scholars, *Except ye become as little children, ye shall not enter into the kingdom of heaven.* The Saviour's *little child*, and the apostle's *fool*, instruct us how to seek heavenly wisdom; not by drawing it from human brains or heathen folios, but by meekly going unto *Jesus* as a *little child* to be taught, or as a fool to be made wise.

What then, you ask, must we cast away the languages, and throw aside the Bible? By no means. Read the word of God with care, and in its native language, if you can; but read it too with prayer; and not with prayer only, but with heart-dependence upon Jesus, while you read. Put your eyes into the Saviour's head, while you look upon his book; and when his head directs your eyes, you will have light enough.

Scribes in every age have been much akin to the Jewish scribes, cavillers at Jesus, and rejecters of his doctrine. They are too wise to be taught, and too lofty to sit down at the feet of Jesus. *God will teach the meek his way. And the wayfaring men, though fools, shall not err.* But *the Lord turneth wise men backward, and maketh their knowledge foolish;* yea, *taketh the wise in their own craftiness.*

Sir, this subject has been often on my thoughts, and much might be said upon it; but this little shall suffice, which perhaps may set all Ephesus in an uproar about their goddess; and make them cry out vehemently, as before, *Great is Diana of the Ephesians.*

Indeed, doctor, I am willing to become a convert here; for the grazier is no scholar, yet endued with common sense. And if scholarship is needful for a Christian, it seemeth *hard* that the poor, who are much the largest part, should be barred from it unavoidably. And it seemeth also *strange*, that the poor should be found and declared the chief subjects of the gospel-kingdom. But, doctor, if Jesus Christ has all the stores I need, and is in heaven; how must I get at him? Astronomers, they say, by a wooden-pipe will spring up to the skies in a twink; and tell as many pretty stories of the stars, as if they had them all in their pocket. I am a gross, unwieldy man, you see; and being born without wings, dare not venture on a flight towards the skies. Can you help me to a ladder, which may conduct me thither?

Yes, sir, you may meet with such a one in Genesis xxviii. 12, whose foot was resting on the earth, while its top was in the skies.

Jacob saw the ladder in a dream, but Jesus gave the vision, to represent himself. The ladder foot, resting on the earth, bespeaks his human nature, as the ladder top, fairly fixed in the skies, denotes his divine nature; and he stood upon the ladder, to point out the emblem. At the incarnation of Jesus, this ladder was truly set up; and much intercourse was then carried on between the family above and the family below: therefore angels are described as descending and ascending on the ladder. And, sir, if Jesus Christ may represent himself by a *door*, why not also by a *ladder*?

Jesus explains the riddle, when he tells Nicodemus, *No man hath ascended up to heaven, but he that came down from heaven, even the Son of man, who* is *in heaven*, is now in heaven by his divine nature, while his human nature, like the ladder's foot, rests on earth. Again, he tells his disciples, *where I am, there shall ye be also.* He does not say, where I *shall* be, there shall ye be also; but where I now *am*, even in heaven by my divine nature, there also shall my servant be.

Doctor, this vision of Jacob may be a very suitable emblem; but I fear it will not help me to the skies. A visionary ladder may suit a light-heeled angel, but will not suit my heavy body. I shall certainly either miss the rounds, or they will break and let me drop; and a fall, only from the moon, would make lamentable work with my carcass. Therefore, unless you can provide me with another ladder, I must grovel still on earth. But does it not seem strange that angels should wait on men? I do not wait upon my servant Tom, though he is my fellow creature. Indeed this service of the angels oft amazeth me.

Sir, God's two families of angels and men, seem by the covenant of grace to be brought into one, and to bear a joint relation to a common head, Christ Jesus. Man, one branch, was cast out of order by the fall of Adam; and angels, the other branch, were in danger of falling, as appears by the ruin of their fellows. Both the families are now brought under one head, and the two branches grafted into a common stock, Christ Jesus. Henceforth they receive all supplies *immediately* from this new head. In him they all unite, on him they all depend for peace and safety. By him angels are preserved from committing sin, and men redeemed from sin committed. Through him angels receive a confirmation in glory, and men obtain admission into glory.

This seems to be St. Paul's meaning when he says, *That in the dispensation* (of grace manifested) *at the full* (or proper) *time, God* (ἀνακεφαλαιώσασθαι) *hath gathered up again, into one head, even Christ, all things which are in heaven, and which are on earth.* Hence, *the whole family in heaven and earth,* (being thus united to Christ) *are named from him.* And as angels are the *chief* or higher branch of the family, they become waiting servants on the lower branch, according to Christ's command, *Whoever will be chief among you, let him become your servant.*

It is not wonderful that angels wait on men, when the Lord of angels came from heaven to wait himself upon them, and to die for them. And this should teach superiors to pay the utmost condescension and the kindest offices to all beneath them. Angels perform this waiting service with cheerfulness, because there is no pride in heaven —that foul weed only groweth upon rotten dunghills.

But, sir, if Jacob's ladder does not suit your purpose, another may be had. My master was a carpenter; he built the skies, and coming down to earth, he took a trade adapted to his work above. He can provide you with another ladder, decked with golden rounds of faith, by which you may ascend up to his seat, and fetch down needful stores.

That is good news, doctor, for I am growing weary of my own ladder. It has been fifty years in my possession, and never raised my heart a single step above the earth. I am just as anxious now about the world as I was, and find no more desire to pray than I used to do; and as for peace passing all understanding, I know no more how it tastes, than of old hock or French burgundy. Pray, inform me of what materials your ladder is composed, and how it differs from the common human one, which every country carpenter can make.

True Christian faith, sir, is of divine origin. It does not grow upon the fallows of nature, nor in the garden of science; neither spruceness of wit, nor solidity of judgment can produce it. An astronomic eye, though vaulting to the stars, cannot reach it; and a metaphysic head, though wrapped deep in clouds, cannot understand it. It is no endowment or acquirement of nature, but *the gift of God* and wrought *by the operation of his Spirit.*

Human faith is only human assent to the word of God, which may be quickly given; so the shield is forged at a single welding, and believers sprout up hastily, like mushrooms. Thus a proselyte who takes a *new creed* becomes a convert instantly; he needs but turn about, just as the wind of fancy blows, and this is called conversion. But he may turn a protestant, a churchman, a methodist, a baptist, a deist, and be zealous too at every turn, while the wind blows, yet never turn to God.

This human faith, sprouting from an helpless mind, can produce no heavenly fruit; but leaves a man just as it found him. Hence it is vilified, as well it may; and none but madmen ever could dream of being saved by this human faith. It takes a quiet lodging in the understanding, and sleepeth there; and being *only* lodged there, a devil may and does possess it.

Doctor, you deal mainly with the devil, but I cannot blame you. Pulpit-lips, like pulpit-cushions, are chiefly lined with velvet. Amazing reverence is shown to Satan in a pulpit; it seems the privy closet of his highness. We never hear his name or habitation mentioned in a modern sermon; which make some people fancy that the devil sure is dead, and that hell-fire is quite burnt out. Nay,

I am told that Jesus Christ did put the devil's name into his short prayer, and called him the *evil one*, but some roguish body wiped his name out from our English translation. However, let that matter pass, and tell me something more about believing. If faith is not a mere human assent to the word of God, what is it, doctor?

Divine faith, sir, takes in this assent to the word of God, but takes in more abundantly. It is described in Scripture by *coming to Jesus* for help, *looking to him* for relief, *flying to him* for refuge, *resting on him* for support, and *feeding on him*, as our heavenly bread. Which expressions not only suppose a credit given to his word by the understanding, but a full reliance of the heart upon him to fulfil his word. The exercise of faith lieth chiefly in the *heart*, as Paul testifies, *With the* heart *man believeth unto righteousness.* Thus faith is not a mere *credit* given to the word of Jesus, but a *heart trust* reposed in him; and therefore called believing *on* him.

The miracles recorded in the Gospel shew the nature and the use of faith; they tell a sinner what his business is with the Saviour, and how he must go to him.

Some came to Jesus for the pardon of sin, and *received* a pardon; others brought diseases, and were healed. Each bodily complaint, brought to Christ, was an emblem of some spiritual disease in our nature, which needs a healing, and can be healed only by the spiritual physician.

The *manner* also of applying for a cure is not recorded as a matter of mere history, but an example for imitation. Every one who went and got a cure calls on you, Sir, to go and do likewise. This matter is important; all are much concerned in it, and a few remarks upon it may be needful.

When the patients went to Christ, they plead no *worthiness* to recommend them. They do not come to *buy* but *beg* a cure. They carry no money in their caps, and bring no merit in their mouths, to purchase blessings, but come as *miserable* creatures, and in a *worshipping* posture, to obtain an act of mercy.

So must you go unto Jesus, if you hope to speed ; feeling yourself a *miserable* sinner, *worshipping* the Saviour, and seeking mercy to relieve your misery. Though in heaven, Jesus Christ is near you, round about you, always within call ; and when your wants are felt, you may go and be healed. Real beggars are relieved now, as aforetime ; for *Jesus is the same yesterday, to-day, and forever ;* but he turns sham-beggars from his door with indignation, just as we do — beggars who can make a bawling of their misery and feel none.

Again, the patients come to Jesus, not as miserable creatures only, but as *helpless* ones, quite unable to relieve themselves. Some had tried human means ; and some had wasted all their substance on those means ; but finding no relief, they come at last to Jesus, and seek a cure from his hand *alone.* Blind Bartimeus does not dream of putting one eye in, while Jesus puts the other ; nor does the leper hope to help the Lord to scour away his leprosy. The patients who applied to Jesus expected *all* their help from him.

So must you apply, if you expect relief ; not vainly dreaming of a power to help yourself, and idly complimenting Jesus with a prayer for help ; not hoping you may couch one eye by human wisdom, while Jesus tries to couch the other; not boasting you can heal some leprous spots yourself, while Jesus scours away the rest. Such haughty beggars meet no relief from Christ: he will be *all* or *nothing*.

Again, the patients came to Jesus, not only as miserable creatures, and helpless, but as *believers*, who thought him able to help, and *expected* help from his mercy. This matter of *believing* was of the utmost consequence, and therefore Jesus usually either asks a patient, before a cure, believest *thou that I am about to do this?* Or tells him after a cure, *thy faith hath saved thee.* And this was said to inform the attending crowd, that faith procured the blessing. For, though a patient's misery and helplessness brought him unto Christ, it was faith alone that obtained the blessing. The patient got what he wanted, by a firm reliance on the power and mercy of this divine physician: *Thy faith hath saved thee.*

Even so it is now, sir. If you desire help from Jesus, you must not seek to him with a vain opinion of your own *worth* to recommend yourself, nor of your own *power* to help yourself, but must place your *whole* dependence on his mercy and his power to save you. Your *whole* expectation of pardon must be from *his blood*, and your *whole* expectation of holiness from *his Spirit*. He *alone* must wash you, and he *alone* must *work in you to will and do*. And if *your eye is single*, singly fixed upon Jesus, he will shew himself a Saviour, and fill you notably with heavenly light and peace.

When you pray to Jesus Christ to save you from the guilt and power of sin, remember, sir, he asks you, by his word, the same question now which he asked aforetime, *Believest thou that I am able to do this?* Not you and I together. No; but believest thou that I—I without you—I *alone*, am able to do this? And till you can answer this question truly, and say, "Lord, I do believe it," your petitions will draw down no blessing.

Many prayers are made, and meet with no success. The petitioners continue slaves to evil tempers and affections, because their petitions are not offered up in faith. Such heathen prayers never reach the skies, but are dropped in a church on a Sunday, swept out on Monday by the sexton, and applied with other rubbish, to cherish some bald grave.

Lastly, when patients came to Jesus, miserable, helpless, and believing, they never would, and never did depart without a cure. Sometimes they were neglected at the first application, and sometimes much discouraged by a seemingly rough answer, but at length their request was granted. And when any met with much discouragement before they gained a blessing, they were dismissed, not with huge encomiums on their honesty, sobriety, and charity (very needful things in their proper place, and might belong to the patients,) but they were sent away with rare commendations of their faith: *O woman, great is thy faith, be it unto thee even as thou wilt.*

And so it is now, sir. All that seek to Jesus Christ, with a due sense of their misery and helplessness, and with a single trust on his power and mercy, will obtain what they seek. They may wait a while at mercy's gate, and meet with some discouragement; but at length it will be opened. The mourners will be comforted with pardons, and weary sinners will find rest unto their souls. Thus the promises, which are only gazed on by others as a fine picture, prove a heavenly feast to them. By faith they are possessed and enjoyed, as they were intended, which brings abundant praise to God.

Once, sir, I went to Jesus, like a coxcomb, and gave myself fine airs, fancying if he was something, so was I; if he had merit, so had I. And, sir, I used him as a healthy man will use a walking staff, lean an ounce upon it, or vapour with it in the air. But now he is my whole crutch, no foot can stir a step without him. He is my all, as he ought to be, if he will become my Saviour; and he bids me *cast*, not *some*, but *all my care upon him.*

My heart can have no rest unless it leans upon him *wholly*, and then it feels his peace. But I am apt to leave my resting-place, and when I ramble from it my heart will quickly brew up mischief. Some evil temper now begins to boil, or some care would fain perplex me, or some idol wants to please me, or some deadness or some lightness creeps upon my spirit, and communion with my Saviour is withdrawn. When these thorns stick in my flesh, I do not try, as heretofore, to pick them out with my own needle, but carry all complaints to Jesus, casting every care upon him. His office is to save, and mine to look for help.

If evil tempers rise, I go to him as some demoniac; if deadness creeps upon me, I go a paralytic; if dissipation comes, I go a lunatic; if darkness clouds my peace, I go a Bartimeus; and when I pray, I always go a leper, crying, as Isaiah did, *Unclean! unclean!*

If but a little faith is mixed with my prayer, which is too oft the case, I get but little help, and find the Lord's word true, *According to your faith it shall be done unto you.* And St. James rebukes me sternly, *Ask in faith*, nothing wavering, *else you shall receive nothing from the Lord.*

Thus the miracles instruct me how to go to Jesus; and every miracle explains the meaning of that general invitation which Jesus gives to sinners—*Come unto me, all ye that labor and are heavy laden, and I will give you rest.* And, sir, unless you come in this appointed way, you will find no more relief from the king of Israel than from the king of Poland.

Indeed, doctor, we have nothing to trouble us in our parish, besides family cares and bodily infirmities. The vicar's chief complaint is about his large family and scanty income; and the old clerk's weekly moan is about his rusty voice, which cannot rear a psalm without a woful outcry. On Sundays we march to church in our best clothes, and are decently seated in pews, which are swept every Christmas. Aged people look grave enough, but the young ones stare about them, and are peeping at every one who steps into the church; for we keep dropping in all prayer-time. And during the sermon, which is soon dispatched, some listen, others giggle; and when the weather waxes warm, a few are half awake, and the rest are dropped asleep; which proves they have no burden. This is our parish way of going unto Jesus Christ; and as for yours, doctor, it seems more suitable for thieves and harlots than for honest folks.

Sir, if it suits a thief and harlot, it will suit you all

exactly. You are robbing God of his service daily, which is the worst of robbery, and yet but little heeded. You defraud your Maker and your hourly benefactor of his worship and obedience, and cannot feel your infamous ingratitude. If a villain takes away your property or good name, you raise an outcry presently; but though you daily rob God of his service and his honor, you can wipe your mouth, and think no harm is done. Your heart too is full of uncleanness; no harlot's heart need be more unclean; and your eye is full as wanton as your heart. Oh, sir, you feel no pain from sin, because your eye is not couched to see your malady, nor your conscience yet alive to feel your danger.

In a Christian land, men become Christians by profession. And while the life is decent, and the church attended, all things pass off mighty well. But it happens, these genteel professors are the very troops of Ezekiel's army, before it was quickened; covered well with plump flesh and fair skin, yet no breath was in them; ranged well in rank and file, bone comes to his bone, and at a distance seem a famous army; but on a near approach are all dead men. No life is found among them, because the Holy Spirit has not breathed upon them.

So it fared in the prophet's day, and so it fareth now. A Christian army still appears, with many decent soldiers of kindly flesh and skin, and, when exercised at church, are ranked well in order; bone comes to his bone, and a *noise* of prayer is heard, but no breath of life is found, no presence of the Lord bestowed, no quickening aids imparted, no cheering consolations granted. It is a dead scene of worship, conducted like an undertaker's funeral with very cloudy face, and yawning entertainment.

It is not strange that men reject the Gospel, when they find no heavenly comfort from it, and are told they must expect none here. Who will labor in a service where he meets with constant drudgery, and no refreshment? Who can bear to be much in prayer, unless he finds divine communion in it, which is divine refreshment? And who will daily read the word of God, unless he finds it daily food? Take the food away, the Spirit's application, and we soon grow weary of the Bible, and the spider weaves his web upon it. Nor is this the worst of all; for some, who live upon the altar, now begin, like Eli's sons, to kick at the sacrifice, and, in a mighty rage of zeal for the Father, would strip his dear Son of divinity, and trample on his blood. When this becomes general, we may expect that Jesus Christ will sweep the church-lands, as he swept the abbey-lands, out of his vineyard; and make our Sion, once a praise in the earth, to become a hissing and an execration.

Well, but doctor, I am not yet satisfied that Jesus Christ must *work all our works in us*, and be both *author and finisher of salvation*. What, cannot I help to make myself a Christian? Is the *government so* wholly *laid upon his shoulders*, that he must do all? You know the old proverb, and proverbs are next to gospel — "Every tub must stand on its own bottom." I would not undervalue Jesus Christ, nor yet disparage myself. At a dead lift I would ask his help; but his arm and my shoulder should act together, and thus raise the sack upon my back.

Sir, your whole *help is laid on him, who is mighty to save, and saves to the uttermost.* He instructs you, by the similitude of a vine and its branches, that all the spiritual life and fruit of a believer is derived from him. Jesus Christ is both the root and stem of this vine. The visible stem may denote his human nature; and the invisible root, producing that stem, his divine nature; and believers are branches of this vine. Now, sir, as all the branches of a vine receive their *birth*, *growth*, and *nourishment*, their wood, leaf, and fruit *altogether* from the vine; so all believers receive their *birth*, *growth*, and *nourishment*, their *life*, *faith*, and *fruit* from Jesus *altogether*. And, sir, if this similitude be good for anything, it proves your will and power are good for nothing—good for nothing but to make a Christian monkey, who will ape a true believer by his chattering.

A branch is nothing, and can do nothing without the vine. If separated from the vine, it dies immediately. Believers too are nothing, and can do nothing without Christ; he is their all in everything; and if they could be separated from him, they would die a spiritual death directly.

Formerly, when I had asked help in prayer, instead of looking for that help, and relying on it, I strove to help myself, and stripped to fight my adversary. Many of these battles I have fought, but never gained any credit by them. My foe would drop his head sometimes by a blow I gave him, and seemed to be expiring, but revived presently, and grew as pert as ever. I found he valued not an arm of flesh, but made a very scornful puff at human will and might. Often when a fire broke out in my bosom, the water I threw on to quench it only proved oil, and made it burn the faster. The flame of anger would continue in my breast till its materials were consumed, or till another fire broke out. One wave of trouble e'erwhile passed over, because another rolled on, and took its place. One evil often drove another out, as lions drive out wolves; but in their turns, my bosom was a prey to every wild beast in the forest. Or if a quiet hour passed, it proved but a dead calm. My heart had no delight in God, a stranger yet to heavenly peace and joy.

At length, after years of fruitless struggling, I was shewn the gospel-method of obtaining rest, not by *working*, but *believing*. A strange and foolish way it seems to nature, and so it seemed to me; but is a most effectual way, because it is the Lord's appointed way.

Jesus says, *He that believeth shall be saved.* Paul declares, *We who have believed do enter into rest.* John affirms, *This is the victory that overcomes the world, even our faith.* And Isaiah bore his testimony long before, that *God would keep the man in perfect peace, whose mind was stayed on him.*

I find my bosom is a troubled sea, and none can give it rest but that God-man, who said to winds and waves, "Be still," and they obeyed his voice. And when I stand before him, as his patients did of old, imploring and expecting help, his help is freely given. *None ever trusted in him and was confounded.*

Fain we would grow notable by *doing;* it suits our legal spirit; but we can grow valiant and successful only by *believing.* When salvation-work is taken on ourselves, it resteth on an arm of flesh, and a withered arm, which must fail; but when we wrestle by believing, the arm of Jesus is engaged to fight the battle; and he will and must bring victory, else his word and faithfulness would fail.

Means of grace are put into my hand, but the *work* is in the Lord's. Watching, praying, and believing do belong to me, and these I must be taught of God, or I shall never do them right; but all deliverance comes from Jesus Christ. And because he does the work, fights the battle, and brings victory, he is rightly called the Saviour. I must watch against the inroads of an enemy; and when he comes in sight, must wrestle well with prayer, and *fight the fight of faith;* but if I thrust my arm into the battle, Jesus will withdraw his own: he will be all or nothing. And if I *lay my hand upon the ark*, to help to hold it up, as Uzza did, I shall be slain, as Uzza was.

The crime of Uzza is but little understood; some think it a slight one, and the punishment severe. But the same sin destroyed Uzza, which destroyeth every sinner, even unbelief. What slew his body, slayeth all the souls that perish. He could not trust the Lord *wholly* with his ark, but must have a meddling finger, called in the Bible-margin, his *rashness*. *Rash* worm indeed to help a God to do his work! and thousands everywhere are guilty of this *rashness*, and perish by this *Uzzaizing*. Jesus Christ is jealous of his glory as Saviour: he will not share it with an other; and whoso takes it from him shall take it at his peril.

The Saviour's word to an Israelite, is, *Fear not, stand still, and see the salvation of God. In* quietness *and* confidence *shall be your strength. Cast thy burden on the Lord, and he shall support thee. Look to* me *for salvation, all the ends of the earth. Call on me in time of trouble,* I will *deliver thee, and thou shalt glorify me.*

A stranger to the life of faith makes a sport about believing, and thinks no work so easy or so trifling. He wonders why such *gentle* business should be called the *fight* of faith; and why the chosen twelve should pray for faith, when every human brain might quickly furnish out a handsome dose.

For my own part, since first my unbelief was felt, I have been praying fifteen years for faith, and praying with some earnestness, and am not yet possessed of more than *half* a grain. You smile, sir, I perceive, at the smallness of the quantity; but you would not if you knew its efficacy. Jesus, who knew it well, assures you that a single grain, and a grain as small as mustard seed, would *remove a mountain;* remove a *mountain*-load of guilt from the conscience, a *mountain*-lust from the heart, and any *mountain*-load of trouble from the mind.

The Gospel law is called the *law of faith*; and Jesus sendeth help according to our faith, and is obliged to send it — not through any merit which is found in faith, but by virtue of his promise, *According to your faith be it unto you.*

This law of faith, or a *whole* reliance upon Christ for *wisdom, righteousness, sanctification,* and *redemption,* is become an exploded doctrine; and human arms are called in to help the Saviour in his work. Salvation is no longer, as St. Paul declares, *by grace through faith,* but by grace and nature *jointly.* And see, sir, what has followed. Morality has lost its right foundation, and is sinking daily, because it resteth on a human shoulder, which cannot bear the weight.

The Gospel too is not only much neglected, but rejected and despised also — a certain consequence of the present modish doctrine. A mixed covenant of human might and heavenly help, will rest at last on human shoulders.

For, observe, preachers say we must ourselves do *something* in salvation-work, but cannot say how *much*. They do not mark the boundary of grace and nature, because they cannot tell what human wit and might may do. Of course every man must make the boundary himself.

One thinks he can do *much;* another can do *more;* and a deist will do *all.* Why should he not? You have put him in the path, and set his feet a going; and you must not be offended if he takes a step beyond you. Perhaps yourself can do with only Christ's shoe-latchet, and he will cast the latchet too away. If your path be right, he may enlarge his step just as he pleaseth; for you cannot mark the ground where he ought to stop.

Thus, when the doctrines of human *merit* or of human *might* are preached, they must naturally, and will judicially end in deism, or a total rejection of the grace of Christ; because no limit can be fixed where that human *merit,* or this human *might* shall end. If Jesus Christ is not *all* in every thing, he will become a cypher.

Paul says, salvation *is of* faith, *that it might be by* grace — that is, we must be saved by faith *alone* in Christ, by a *whole* dependence upon him for every thing, otherwise salvation cannot be by grace, cannot be a *mere* matter of grace. If men retain some native will and power to save themselves, and exercise it properly, so far they are saved, not by dependence upon Jesus, but by a proper exercise of their own abilities. Adam was endowed with native will and power to save himself, and had he persevered in a right use of those powers, he would not have been saved by grace at all, but by works altogether. And if fallen man has yet some power to save himself, and makes a proper use thereof, so far he is saved by his own works; but then, says Paul, pray what becomes of grace? If you are truly saved by grace, it must be through faith alone. Your whole dependence must be fixed on Jesus, and your obligations rise entirely from him, else you are not saved by grace. What you can do for yourself, you need not be obliged to another for; no grace is wanted here.

And as salvation, in a covenant of grace, must be through faith alone, so that covenant supposes that we want such grace, for God will offer nothing needlessly, not even grace.

A fallen man has no more power than a fallen angel to sanctify his nature, or to make atonement for sin. Man fell through pride, as angels did; and to humble man in his recovery, he must go clean out of himself for salvation. His *whole* dependence must be on the Saviour's blood for pardon, and on the Saviour's grace for holiness. Therefore Jesus saith, *Look to me, and be saved.*

But, sir, a little recollection how it fares with yourself and neighbors would save a deal of talking on this matter. You are an aged man, and seem an honest man, and must have tried what human strength can do. Are your tongue and temper better bridled than they were some forty years ago? Can you love and feed an enemy much better? Can you deal your bread more freely to the hungry; and more cheerfully submit to sickness, pain, and worldly disappointments? Are you growing more humble, and more vile in your own eyes? Can you pray more frequently and fervently, and walk with God more closely, and find the comfort of his presence? Is the word of God more read, and read with sweeter savor? Can you keep a stricter watch upon your bosom, and find more power over bosom-sins? Is your *cage* more cleanly, and your *den* well scoured? Survey yourself all over, then call upon your neighbors, and ask them all the same questions, and see what answers they will make. I fear you will find no great amendment, and can have no room to vaunt of human strength, but abundant room for self-condemnation.

As for the tub you mentioned, it has lost its bottom, sir, above five thousand years; and it would be strange indeed if it stood upon a bottom when it had none. Adam has unbottomed all our vessels, and left us no foundation to rest upon but Jesus Christ. Adam fell, and ruined all his race.

Indeed, doctor, I have the vanity to think myself as good a man as Adam was before he fell. Why should his fall put my nose out of joint? Could he not stumble without throwing me down? Perhaps, he did receive a bruise, and his ankle might be sprained, but I do not read that he broke his neck, or broke a leg, by the fall. Does the Scripture intimate that his whole nature was impaired, and that he fell from his *first estate* altogether.

So I think, sir, but hear and judge. The Lord tells

Adam, *In the day he eateth he shall* surely *die.* Adam did eat of the tree, and of course he *died* on the day he ate, if the word of God is true and faithful. But what death did Adam die on the day he ate? Not a natural, but a spiritual death. All spiritual life ceased on the day he sinned, and his soul was *dead* to God. His animal life became a sickly and a mortal one, and the spiritual life expired in him, as in the sinning angels.

To fancy that mere mortality was only meant by the threatening, is a strange perversion of God's awful sentence, which does not say, *Thou shalt be liable to death,* but *thou shalt* surely *die.*

Adam lived nine hundred years after his transgression, and might have lived nine millions, consistently enough with mere mortality, but not with the threatening. And if one expositor may add the word *liable* to the threatening, in order to shove it from the spirit, why may not another add the little word *not,* to shove it from the body too? So the threatening runs thus — *In the day thou eatest, thou shalt* not *be liable to death;* and all is safe and well. The threatening proveth only papal thunder.

But why must all the threatening light upon the body, and the curse be spent upon it altogether? The whole nature sinned, and the whole should suffer. The body lost its healthy state, and the spirit sure should lose its healthy state too. Nay, the spirit was the *chief* in transgression, and should bear the *chief* share of punishment. If the body grew sickly through sin, the soul should be sick to *death.* When a gang of thieves is taken, the captain of the gang is sure to suffer, whatever happens to the rest. But here the captain in rebellion is reprieved, and the underling is hanged: the spirit strangely escapes without a hurt, and the curse falls wholly on the poor body.

The change of Adam's *state* is pointed out by the following circumstances: —

1. After the fall he desired no fellowship with God, but dreaded it. When the Lord calls, he flies, and would avoid all converse with him. The language of his heart was this, "Depart from me, I desire no knowledge of thee, or communion with thee."

2. His *understanding* now was clouded, and a spiritual darkness crept upon it. He has lost the right knowledge of God, and thinks his Maker sees with human eyes, or useth spectacles. For he is no sooner called but he slips behind a tree, as a mouse will slip behind a tile, to hide himself.

3. His *breast* was now become the seat of evil tempers, such as devils feel; and felt as Adam did, through disobedience. Their bosoms once, like his, were the blessed seat of heavenly peace, and love, and joy; but when sin entered, they became a woful seat of war, where wrath and envy, pride and stubbornness, and every evil temper reign. Adam shews this devilish bosom, when examined; for though examined with much tenderness, he makes no meek confession, nor deigns to urge a single prayer for mercy. He acts a stubborn part, flies in the face of God, and dares to lay the blame at his Maker's door, as if the woman had been made on purpose to seduce him: *The woman whom thou gavest me, she gave me of the tree.*

4. Adam's *heart*, through sin, became a cage of all uncleanness. Before his fall he felt no shame, though naked; but when he fell, such filthy lusts sprung up, as

brought him shame enough, and made him seek a covering for his person.

5. Adam's first-born child proves a murderer. A hopeful heir, truly! Where the fruit shows the stock, and declares them both possessed of *his* nature, who is called a *murderer from the beginning.* And if St. John is credited, that *whoso hates his brother is a murderer*, then every child of Adam, in his turn, has been a murderer too.

Now, sir, we may debate the point a little. If angels lost their *first estate* by sin, it is not wonderful that man should lose it. If Adam had not lost it, would God act consistently in his moral government? God must hate sin in Adam, as well as in an angel, because it is evermore that abominable thing which he loatheth — that accursed thing which he hateth. And his declarations concerning sin are these, which are very awful, and must be universal, *The wages of sin is death;* and *the soul that sinneth, it shall die.* The angels sinned, and, being spirits, had no earthly case, like ours, to become mortal; but they underwent a spiritual death, and became dead to God. All communion with God ceased; the heavenly image was withdrawn, and the devilish nature introduced.

Sin is just the same deadly bane to the spirit that poison is to the body: a single dose does the business. Angels lost their *first estate* by this poison of sin; and if disobedience required a *change* of *state* in angels, it must require the same in man. For God acts uniformly in his moral government: he is Jehovah, and *changeth not.*

Reasons may be found why God provides a remedy for *fallen men*, and not for *fallen angels;* but no good reason can be given why man should *keep* his first estate after sin committed. Man had a share of the devil's disobedience, and man must have a share of the devil's nature. And enough of this horrid nature is apparent in ourselves and others to confirm the argument.

Some fancy that mortality makes the change of Adam's state; but this is not the whole, nor the chief change; it does not bring the devil's nature, and make us like him. Sickness, pain, and death, are only parts of the curse, which respect the body: the spirit also sinned, and the spirit is afflicted with the devil's nature. Hence Satan is styled *the prince of this world*, because he reigneth in the hearts of men. A devilish prince suits a devilish subject — like loves its like. And *the whole world* are said to *lie in the wicked one*, ἐν τῷ πονηρῷ.

It is not strange that some deny the fall. This is part of that spiritual blindness which has crept upon the understanding, and is just what happens to delirious people in a fever, who fancy they are well, and mock at physic and physician. I make no doubt but the devils, through that pride which accompanieth sin, think as highly of themselves as of the angels. And since they never can repent, they will rather charge their misery to the undeserved wrath of God than to their own iniquity.

Every wicked temper that is found in a fiend I can find in myself, and discern in others. And I could as soon suppose that God created fiends, as believe that he created man in his present state. Before the fall, man was pronounced good — *very good;* but after the fall he became bad indeed — bad enough to be called of God the *devil's child* and the *devil's subject.* Sure Beelzebub must grin to hear his vanquished subjects preach of the dignity of human nature; and if such dignity is found in the subject, how much more in the prince? He may well be honored, like the Turk, his cousin, with the title of *sublime highness.*

Every dog that barks at me, and every horse that lifts his heel against me, proves I am a *fallen* creature. The brute creation durst not shew an enmity before the fall, nor had they any, but testified a willing homage unto Adam, by *coming for a name.* Eve no more dreads the serpent than we dread a fly. But, when man shook off allegiance from his God, the beasts, by divine permission, shook off allegiance too from man.

Where sin enters, pride will enter too, and supply the place of real honor; and as iniquity aboundeth, pride aboundeth also. Else, how could *sinners* boast of *dignity,* and take up mighty state, on account of verbal titles, or of transient manors, when they themselves must presently be eaten up with worms?

Thus, sir, by disobedience, Adam became both a *condemned* sinner, and an *unclean* creature. He was *dead in law* by his trespass, and *dead to God* by his sinful nature; *dead both in trespasses and sins.* The fountain being thus polluted, all its streams were filthy, For *who can bring a clean thing out of that which is* unclean? *Not one.* Hence all are called *children of wrath by nature,* and declared to be *dead in sins.*

Some traces of the moral law remain, producing what we call the moral sense, or conscience; and the lamp of reason burns, though with a dimmer light, yet sufficient to direct our worldly matters; but the spiritual life is quenched. We are *born of the flesh* — born with a *carnal mind which is at enmity with God;* and nothing suits us well but what is pleasing to the flesh. Spiritual service is a shackle put upon the mind, and when the heart is collared with devotion, it drudges through it very heavily, and is mighty froward in it; stops short, starts back, flies out right and left, looks a hundred ways at once, and keeps lowing for the world all the time, just like the two Philistine cows, which drew the Lord's ark to Bethshemesh; they were yoked fast together, and drew forward, but kept lowing for their calves all the while; and though engaged in *religious draught,* both of them fell a sacrifice at Bethshemesh, were slaughtered, quartered, and consumed by fire. An awful type of the end of those who find God's worship not a pleasant service, but *religious draught.*

Now, sir, all mankind abide in this state of death, Heathens, Jews, and Christians, till they are *born of God's Spirit*, and *have his Holy Spirit dwelling in them.* And during their continuance in this state, they neither are, nor can be sensible of it, because it is a state of death, which seals up all *perception.* A dead soul knows no more of its dead condition than a dead body does. Men will mistake a *decent* worship, and a *decent* conduct for the spiritual life, and will suppose that gluttons, drunkards, whoremongers, &c., are the only people in the state of *flesh.* Whereas, St. Jude calls every man a *sensual* man, *who has not the Spirit.*

An experimental knowledge of the Holy Spirit's influence, was the Christian touchstone in St. Paul's day, but modern gospellers have learned a pleasant trick to have the Holy Spirit, yet know nothing of it; and they ask a true believer scornfully, as once a taunting prophet asked Micaiah, *Which way went the Spirit of God from me, to speak to thee?* Did he pop upon you through the key-hole, or through a chink in the wall? Which way, Micaiah, was it? and then *smote him on the cheek.* See here the character of a false prophet, deliniated by the Spirit of truth. He has not the Spirit of God, yet pretends unto it, by saying, Which way went the Spirit *from me?* and he ridicules the Spirit's *sensible* operation, by asking scornfully, *Which way* went the Spirit unto thee? Did you see him come, or feel him come into you, any way? Pray, what way was it? Let us hear, Micaiah, and take this smite upon the cheek for your trouble. Such was the language of false prophets in old time; and where Satan rules, these taunting prophets never die. But, sir, if you have never felt the spiritual death I am speaking of, you are yet a *dead soul*; and will remain so, till Jesus Christ has quickened you.

For as men cannot be sensible of this death, while they abide in it, so neither can they help themselves out of it. Death strips away all *power*, as well as all *perception.* A dead body may as well restore itself to life as a dead soul. A fallen angel may as soon rekindle spiritual life and regain his first estate, as a fallen man. Nothing can produce the spiritual life and a spiritual mind resulting from it, but the Spirit of God. His breath alone brings this life, which Jesus intimates, when he *breathed* upon his disciples, and said, *Receive ye the Holy Ghost.*

Yet, while men are without this life, and walk the rounds of moral decency, they bravely talk of will and power to make themselves the sons of God; and think St. John a mere driveling, for affirming they are born, *not of the* will *of man, but of God.*

A real Christian, in St. Paul's account, is a *new creation.* He is God's *workmanship, created in Christ Jesus.* And Jesus tells you how dead souls are quickened; mark his words; they come with double seal, to shew their weight and certainty. *Verily, verily, I say unto you, the hour is coming, and now* is, *when the dead shall hear the voice of the Son of God, and they that hear shall live.* Jesus is not speaking of the body's resurrection at the judgment-day, but a resurrection, which *now is,* and is *coming* every day—a resurrection of dead souls to life, not a merely moral, but a spiritual life; and a resurrection caused, not by us, but by himself, even by his *voice.* He has many voices to call dead sinners by, the voice of his word, of his servants, and his providences; but all these avail nothing, without the voice of his *Spirit.* His word is but a dead letter without the quickening Spirit: his servants are but barking dogs, who growl, yet cannot bite, unless he set them on; and his providences are but claps of thunder, alarming for a time, yet quickly over, except he rides himself upon the storm. When he takes the work into his own hand, and the voice of his Spirit accompanies the voice of his word, or his servants, or his providences, then a sinner hears, and starts from his grave, like Lazarus, and lives. And having thus received life, he feels his condemnation and his ruined nature, and crieth after Jesus.

When the world was brought into this ruined state by sin, man could do nothing more to help himself than the fallen angels could, and must perish everlastingly, unless the Lord make bare his arm. He does, and provides another covenant; the stores of which are not laid up in Adam, as before, nor in his ruined children. God does not choose to trust a bankrupt. If man could not stand upright, when set upon his legs, how shall he stand when he has none? Therefore *help is now laid upon one who is mighty and able to save to the uttermost.* And the Saviour thus bespeaks the ruined sinner, *Thou hast* destroyed *thyself, but* in me *is thy help.*

However, though man fell, God was not disappointed by his fall; it was foreseen: for, *known to God are all his works from the beginning*, and, being foreseen, it was provided against in such a manner as might exalt the riches of his grace in man's recovery. The first covenant was made with Adam, a mere man, who was the surety of it; but the surety failed and ruined all. The second covenant was not made with the ruined sinner, a broken merchant, but with Jesus Christ, the Lord from heaven. Jehovah says, *I give* thee *for a covenant*, and of course, *Jesus is the surety of this better covenant.*

Now the business of a surety is to pay the *legal debts* of another. Our legal debts are, first, *perfect obedience*, which alone can bring a *title* unto heaven; secondly, the *curse of death*, for not performing that obedience.

Jesus Christ first pays the debt of perfect obedience; and thereby, as surety, redeems the heavenly title; then he takes the law-curse on himself, to free believers from it. And both these blessings are *imputed*, or charged to the account of every true believer. By the death of his surety he is freed from condemnation; and by *his alone obedience he is made righteous*, justified in the eye of the law, and obtains a *legal title* unto heaven.

And, sir, there is nothing monstrous in this matter, however some may please to startle at it. Human laws every where, as well as the divine, allow of suretyship; which proves it is an equitable thing. If farmer Thomas does some common work for farmer James, the law *imputes* the work done by Thomas unto James. When a curate preaches for a weary rector, the law *imputes* the curate's mouth to the silent rector. If you were overwhelmed with debts and friendly surety did discharge them all, the law would *impute* this payment unto you, and acquit you of debt as effectually, as if the money had been taken from your own purse, and paid with your own hand.

Indeed, though suretyship is common among men in debts of *money*, it is not practiced in debts of *life*. For who will die for another? A rogue will not thrust his neck into the halter for a rogue; and an honest man would not choose it, nor might the state consent unto it; for honest men are scarce. But the law itself has no abhorrence of such suretyship, and would gain abundant reverence by it.

When a villain dies by the hand of justice, we attend more to the *guilt* of the sufferer, and to our own *security* by his death, than to the *honor* which the law receives by his execution. But if an upright man, and well esteemed, should freely suffer for a villain, this striking spectacle would bring much *reverence* to the law, and give it great *solemnity*.

Zaleucus, a prince of the Locrians, made a law, that

every one convicted of adultery should lose both his eyes, and it happened that his own son was convicted of the crime. The prince was not willing that the law should lose its honor, nor could the father bear to see his son quite blind. He therefore orders one of his own eyes to be bored out, and one of his son's. Thus two eyes were given to the law, which brought it more solemnity than if the son had lost both his own. In such a case, as he passed along, many might have cried—"There goes the blind youth, who could not let his neighbor's wife alone." But when the aged father stirs abroad, and is seen with an eye dug out, this sight of suffering innocence strikes beholders' hearts with awe, and makes them reverence the law, and dread adultery.

Pray, hold your hand a little, doctor, every honest man will strive to pay his debts, and if he cannot pay the whole, will make a composition, and pay what he can. Such a composition I would make for my sinful debts, and should hope to pay ten shillings in the pound, or a better penny. I am not so vain as to reject a surety altogether, relying wholly on my own ability for payment, nor can I think myself quite insolvent. I would therefore have the old grazier and Jesus Christ jointly bound in the same bond. This would look creditable, and I could condescend to let the Saviour sign his name first, though I paid full fifteen shillings in the pound. What think you of this, doctor?

Sir, I think such a bond would dishonor Christ, and ruin you effectually. If you fancy God's authority is a trifling business, and does not need a surety to make *whole* satisfaction for sin, you would do well to consider what has happened to the fallen angels, for want of such a surety. They sinned; and the trespass, which brought on their punishment, was a single one, no doubt, like Adam's. For, in God's government, *The wages of* every *sin is death.* Yet their single trespass has cast them out of heaven, cursed them with a devilish nature, and doomed them to everlasting misery.

You may thrust your name into the covenant, if you please, as a joint-bondsman, but it will be at your utter peril; for the Father and the Son will both reject you with abhorrence. The Father has provided a surety for this better covenant — a *sufficient* surety, and named him *singly*, and thereby has excluded every other. And if you foist your own name into the covenant, as a joint-bondsman, to discharge your debts, what is this but reflecting on the wisdom of the Father, as if he knew not how to provide a surety; and on the power of the Son, as if he was not able to execute his office? Sir, this is horrible presumption, and will find a proper recompense at a proper time. God will avenge himself of such proud adversaries.

Adam, though a mere man, was qualified, as a surety, to *pay obedience* for all in his loins; yet none but a God-man is qualified to *make atonement* for disobedience. No created being can make any satisfaction unto God for sin; the utmost he can do is to pay his hourly debts, and if the debts are hourly paid, he is still *unprofitable*, has no merit, nor deserveth even thanks; he has only done his duty.

You have read what Jesus says, and what he says is true of *every creature*, angel or man: *When ye have done* all things *which are commanded you, say, we are* unprofitable *servants, we have only done our duty. And does the Lord then thank that servant, who has done the things that were commanded! I suppose not.* You do not thank your own servant for doing what he is commanded, and yet are more obliged to him, a million times, than your Maker is to you. Now, sir, if after having done all our duty, we are yet unprofitable, and unworthy of the smallest thanks, pray, what room is left for merit to make atonement?

This saucy idol cannot show its face in heaven; no angel dares to think of merit. With *two wings he flies,* to shew his swift obedience; with *two, his feet are covered,* to hide obedience from his eyes; and with *two, his face is veiled,* in token of unworthiness. Angels do not *vaunt,* as sinful mortals do, of their obedience and holiness; but with adoring wonder cry, *Holy, holy, holy, is the Lord of hosts!* and pay eternal adoration to this holy *Three,* the *Holy* Father, *Holy* Son, and *Holy* Ghost.

Merit is the fuz-ball, which sprouteth from a dunghill, with a powdered cap; and only garnisheth the crest of sinners, who are daily doing what they ought not, or leaving undone what they ought to do. And if the real wages due to sin is death, then a sinner's merit, and a sinner's dignity, are just of as much value, and just as great a contradiction, as a traitor's loyalty.

If Jesus Christ is a mere creature, though the head of all creation, and had paid most rigorous and sinless obedience, he could only say at last, I have done my duty, and deserve no thanks; I am yet unprofitable, and can plead no merit for myself, much less for others.

But if Jesus Christ is God, he is no more bound to

keep the creature's law than an earthly master is to do his servant's work. And if he pleased to take man's nature, to become man's surety; though the human nature, being but a creature, and acting as a servant, could merit nothing, the divine nature, joined to it by a personal union, can merit, and make noble satisfaction.

The law had claims of obedience upon the human nature of Christ, because it is a creature; but had none upon the divine; it is the Lawgiver, whose word created all things, and whose will gives law to all. Here merit will arise, by doing that service which it was not bound to do.

If your servant does his daily work faithfully, no daily thanks are given nor expected; he only does his duty. But if a neighbor lends a helping hand freely, he merits thanks, because the service was not due from him, but freely offered by him. We may merit from each other, but can merit nothing from the Lord, because our utmost service is ever due to him.

Thus, by the obedience and death of this God-man surety, *the law was magnified and honored* — more honored, than if all the sinful race of men had fallen under its eternal curse for disobedience.

If man had paid a perfect unsinning obedience, it would have been his *title* to heaven — a title founded, not on human merit, but on the Lord's *free promise*, *This do, and thou shalt live.* Without such promise, God might have dropped his creature into nothing, after a thousand years of complete obedience. Yes, if no promise hindered, God might drop a perfect angel into nothing; and perhaps with more justice than we may kill a happy fly, because of his whizzing. Such an angel lives on courtesy and has no reason to complain if it is withdrawn. While he pays obedience, his life abounds with comforts; all things suited to his state are given; but he may drop into nothing, as he was before, if the Lord pleaseth. God was under no obligation to give him life; and without a promise, he is under none to prolong his life; and, least of all, to advance a *human* creature to a *better* life.

The Popish conclave has acted craftily, and more consistently than Protestant divines, by inventing works of *supererogation*. For though these works are false, absurd, and blasphemous, yet, being once allowed, they lay a right foundation for human merit. If a man can do more than he is in duty bound to do, he may merit by such doing. And nothing now is wanted for the Pope, but a Cyclop's eye of infallibility, which any Vulcan readily will make, to determine what these works of supererogation are, and the church's coffers are loaded presently with treasure. Simeon Stylites, by perching on a pillar for a month, shall purchase pardons for a thousand sodomites.

But, sir, we will take leave of the Pope's eye, and proceed. Every man has sinned, and has lost his heavenly *title*. A *single* trespass forfeits it in man or angel, and forfeits it forever. Jesus Christ steps in, as the human surety, and pays the legal debt of *perfect obedience*, and thus *redeems* the sinner's title. Hence, he is called *the Lord our righteousness*. Jesus says himself *Their righteousness is of* me; and the church replies, *In the Lord have I righteousness*. Paul says, *Christ is made* to, or rather for, *us righteousness*, and declares, *We are made righteousness* in *him*, which he calls the righteousness of God, because it was wrought out by the God-man surety.

When John refused baptism unto Jesus, he received this answer, *Suffer it to be so now, for thus it* becomes *us to fulfil* all *righteousness.* Jesus, as the *holy one* of Israel, needed not the laver of baptism; but as Israel's *surety*, he did need it. It *became* him, as surety, to fulfil *all* righteousness, moral and ritual, respecting Jews and Christians. On this account he was both circumcised and baptized, partook of the Jewish passover and the Christian eucharist, and went to the yearly feasts at Jerusalem, as the law required. If a single rite had been neglected, he would not fulfil *all* righteousness, nor could have been a legal surety. A trip in one point would have spoiled all.

But, sir, man has not only forfeited his heavenly title by sin, he has incurred a law-curse too, the curse of eternal death. Sin has both barred heaven's gate against him, and opened hell's gate for him. Now, Jesus Christ, as man's surety, paid this legal debt too. *He was made a curse for us, and* redeemed *us from the curse.*

Paul is in rapture about this love of Christ; and so is every one who feels the blessings purchased by it. Yet how little is this love regarded by modern gospellers! Who bears a dying Saviour on his heart and thinks or talks about him? A melancholy proof of man's fallen nature, of his deep ingratitude and folly. Sure, we must outmatch a devil here! His heart would leap for joy to hear the tidings of a surety; yet men will pass the surety by, some with no regard, and some with much contempt.

Thus Jesus sets the fallen sinner on his legs again, pays

the law-debt of complete obedience to redeem our title, then takes the law-curse on himself to free us from it.

Why, doctor, this is charming news indeed; but if this be all that is needful for salvation, I do not see how any can miscarry. Satan may as well bar up his gates, he will not catch a single straggler. My neighbor *Fillpot*, who comes reeling home at night from the tavern, stands as good a chance as the grazier, who goes soberly to bed. How is this, doctor? Methinks I do not like it, that *Ned Fillpot* should stagger after me to heaven, and get perhaps as good a crown as myself. This will never do. Something surely must be wrought *in* us, as well as something done *for* us.

True, sir, much must be wrought *in* us, not indeed to purchase salvation, which is already purchased by the surety, but to dispose and enable us to receive salvation *freely*, and behave *suitably* for it. Jesus Christ has not only redeemed us from the curse, and bought our title, but has also purchased grace to sanctify our nature, and thereby give us *meetness* for glory. This grace is always given to the heirs of glory, to prepare them for it; and the benefits of Christ's obedience in life and death are made over to them, and sealed on the conscience by the Holy Spirit. Thus they have an inward witness of deliverance from the curse, with a legal title unto heaven, and a gospel-meetness for it. This meetness springs from regeneration, or a spiritual life begun and carried on in the soul, as a preparation for the spiritual worship of heaven. And the spiritual life differs from the merely moral one, as animal motion differs from mechanic motion, or as a man's walking differs from a clock's going. The clock may go *well*, but has not animal life ; and a man may walk *well*, yet have no spiritual life.

Now, sir, observe the case of mere professors. They talk of honesty and decency, and feed upon their withered moral skeleton ; but know not how to *eat the flesh and drink the blood of Christ.* An application of the gospel blessings to their heart is neither sought nor wanted. They hear that Jesus Christ has died, and are satisfied with this report; but his blood, the virtue of it, must be sprinkled on the conscience, or it avails them nothing, will bring them neither gospel-peace nor gospel-holiness. Paul and Peter speak of the *sprinkling of this blood* ; and through this sprinkling, the atonement is *received* by a sinner, and his heart is sweetly drawn to love and follow Jesus. Nothing but partaking of Christ's blessing will effectually engage the heart to Christ. Then he *draws us with the cords of a man,* and *the love of Christ constrains us.*

All the blessings of salvation have been purchased by Jesus, and are at his disposal. He gives them when and where and how he pleases. And do not you expect, sir, to dispose of freely, what you have bought fairly? Jesus saith, *I* give *eternal life unto them ;* and what is freer than a *gift ?* and lest you should think him a usurper, he declares, and pray observe his declaration, *All things are delivered unto me by my Father. All persons*, and *all blessings*, temporal and spiritual, are at *my disposal,* surrendered into my hands by the Father, on account of my undertaking the work of mediator.

So Jesus reigneth, in his human nature, king supreme, disposing of all persons and all blessings, as he pleaseth ;

and must reign, till *all his foes are made his footstool.* Then the kingdom will be administered as before, not by the hand of this God-man mediator, but God the three-one God, will be all in all. In the meantime, Jesus calls and *quickens whom he will*, gives repentance and faith, bestows pardon and justification, affords grace to sanctify believers, and perseverance to bring them safe to glory. Thus the faithful say with David, *Salvation is of the Lord;* and sing hosannahs, not to their own wisdom, strength, or merit, but to *God and the Lamb forever.*

Indeed, doctor, I must cudgel you; I can hold no longer. My patience is worn down to its stump, and the stump is going. What a cypher you make of the poor grazier; and what a hobby-horse of human nature! According to your account, she has no more eyes, ears, or hands to help herself than an oyster. Why, your picture of nature is so horrid black, it would even fright a chimney-sweeper! What? have I no power in myself to begin the christian life, and, when begun, no strength to carry it on? Am I in debt to Jesus Christ for everything?

Please to drop your cudgel, sir, and I will give an answer. A vaporing staff does not suit my fancy. You are indebted unto Christ for every good you do possess, and to yourself for all the evil you commit. Jesus Christ is the author and finisher of every good thing in the spiritual, rational, and animal life; he is alpha and omega in them all.

No animal has life till he gives it; and no animal has power, when in life, to prolong its life a moment. It may eat and drink, yet food and liquor are not life, but means of life. *We live not by bread alone, but by the Word of*

God. That word which bringeth food must give it blessing, and then it nourisheth.

When Christ creates an idiot, all the schools in the world cannot give him reason, because he is born without it.

And where a rational nature is given, and means used for its cultivation, still they are but means, which profit some, and help not others, though alike diligent. Every opening of the understanding, every improvement in science, and every invention in handicrafts, with all skill in working, come *wholly* from Jesus, who is called the *light of men;* and calls himself the *light of the world.* He opens a budding understanding as he opens a budding rose.

Whatever light men have, it proceeds from Christ *alone;* and he can give this light gradually, or give it all at once, as he did to Adam, and as he did to Bezaleel and Aholiab, two brickmakers, who were furnished immediately with *wisdom* of heart, and *skill* of hand, for engraving, carving, embroidering, and all kind of work.

He can make men forget their native language, and speak divers others, in a moment, as he did at Babel; or he can make men retain their native language, and speak divers others, in a moment, as he did at Pentecost.

Courage, too, proceeds from Jesus. When he would exalt a nation, *five of them shall chase an hundred;* and when he would depress a nation, *They shall fly, when none pursueth.*

Neither has a rational nature any power to preserve itself. A philosopher, engaged in study, and surrounded with literature, may turn an idiot, or fall distracted, in a moment; and he would do so, if not supported secretly by Jesus; *his visitation preserveth our spirit.*

Where the animal and rational natures are given, a man is yet void of life spiritual, till Jesus Christ bestows it; as void of life spiritual, as an idiot is of life rational. And as none but Jesus could give an idiot rational life, so none but he can give a rational man spiritual life.

This life was lost at the fall, and never is recovered, till Jesus quickens us. And till this life is recovered, men are only Christian ghosts, having semblance without substance, resting on a *broken* bed of duties, and will find as much relief from it as a hungry stomach from a painted feast.

Paul, I suppose, alludes to the spiritual life when writing to a christian church, styled elsewhere *spiritual men*; he prays that *spirit, soul, and body may be preserved blameless*, which *three* portions make up what he calls the ὁλόκληρον of a christian man, or the *whole lot* of nature assigned him by the Lord.

When spiritual life is given, a man is said to be *born of the Spirit*, and finds divine communion through the Spirit; but has no power in himself to preserve the life which is begun: no more power to continue or enlarge his spiritual life, than his rational or animal life. Means of grace must be used, but these are nothing more than means still. The support, increase, and continuance of the spiritual life are *wholly* from Jesus, *in whom we live and move and have our being.*

Why, doctor, you talk most amazingly of Jesus Christ. I never heard the like before. Some people only vamp him up as a prophet, and trample on his blood; and some, who do not like to hear of hell, shew a Jewish heart, and call him an impostor; but you make him God almighty, our Creator, and Preserver and Redeemer. Truly, I would give him all his due, but must have his honors fetched from the holy Bible, and not from human brains. My besom sweeps away all cobwebs, when spun by a spider or the doctor. Give me some fair and plain account of Jesus Christ from the Scriptures. I love the Bible and can credit what it says.

Now you talk like a man, sir. When you lifted up your staff before, I began to think of packing up my alls. A cudgel is too hard an argument for me. But since you ask for the Bible, I am well content to stay, and tell you what it says of Jesus Christ. Before he had a human nature, he created all things by his divine power, all matter, and all animals, and all spirits, human and angelic. St. John says, *All things were made by him;* and Paul enlarges on St. John's words, saying, *All things were created by him, that are in heaven and that are in earth, visible and invisible:* all things *were created* by *him, and* for *him* — that is, by his *power*, and for his *glory*. Where his Godhead is equally proclaimed by his *creating* power, and by creating all things for his *glory*. Now, sir, if Jesus Christ created all things, he cannot be a creature; otherwise he must create himself, and so have had existence, before he had a being.

Paul goes on and says, *Jesus Christ* is *before all things*. Grammar rules required him to says, Jesus *was* before all things; but he breaks his well known grammar rules, and says, he *is* before all things, to shew his eternal unchangeable existence; and Jesus did the very same, when he said, *Before Abraham was, I am.*

Paul adds further, *By him all things do consist. All things* material, human, or angelic are held together, stand fast, and sustained by him. And again *Jesus upholdeth* all things *by the word of his power.*

Paul sufficiently declares the divinity of Christ, by calling him *the* express *image of the Father's person.* As the impression of a seal on wax exactly answers to the seal itself, line for line, and is the express image of the seal, even so is the Son the express image of the Father. Whatever line of divinity is drawn on the Father, the same is impressed on the Son. Whatever wisdom, power, justice, truth, patience, kindness, mercy, &c., are found in the Father, the same must be found *equally* in the Son, else he is not the *express* image of the Father's person. If any attribute is in the Father which is not in the Son, or is possessed more perfectly by the Father than by the Son, then the Son is not the *express* image of the Father.

Paul asserts that *all the fulness of the Godhead dwelt in Christ bodily;* that is, the divine nature of Jesus, containing *all the fulness of the Godhead,* dwelt in his body, and inhabited it as a temple, just as the Shekinah, or glorious presence of God, inhabited the holy of holies in the first Jerusalem temple; which temple was a type of the body of Christ.

Jesus saith, *All things whatsoever the Father hath are mine,* do belong to me also.

Again he saith, *I and the Father are one,* not one *person,* but one *thing,* one nature, one substance, one essence.

He further affirms, *No one knoweth the Son but the Father, neither knoweth any one the Father but the Son.*

The divine understanding of the Son and the Father are equal and reciprocal—alike infinite in both.

On these accounts, Jesus declares, *Whoso hath seen me hath seen the Father.* My divine nature expressly bears the *essential* image of the Father; and as God-man, I am his *manifestative* image, a visible representative of Jehovah, displaying his divine perfections in such a manner by my words and works, that whoso seeth me hath, in effect, seen the Father. Nothing more is found in him than in myself: *whatsoever he possesseth, I possess.*

The Father himself, speaking to the Son, saith, *Thy throne, O God, is for ever and ever.* And could the Son speak to the Father in more lofty language.

John calls him absolutely, *God who made the world;* the *true God*; and extols his love to mankind by saying, *Hereby perceive we the love of God, because he laid down his life for us.*

Paul says, *He was God manifested in the flesh;* and affirms, that *according to the flesh*, cr his human nature, he sprung from the fathers of the Jewish nation; but in his other nature, was God *over all, blessed forever;* and ratifies the assertion by a solemn *Amen.*

Thomas calls him *my Lord and my God;* and is commended for his faith; but others are commended more who should thus believe on him, though they have not seen him.

Isaiah calls him, *The mighty God; a just God and a Saviour*, who says, *Look unto me, and be saved.*

Jude calls him the *only wise God, our Saviour.* And he is called the *only* wise God, not to exclude the Father and Spirit from an equal share of divinity, but to exclude every one *who is not by nature God.* So when Jesus saith, *no one knoweth the Father, but the Son,* he does not mean to exclude the Holy Ghost, who is by nature God; for *the Spirit searches all things, yea the deep things of God.* And in this sense we say to Christ in our communion service, "Thou *only* art holy," not intending to exclude the Father and the Spirit from this holiness, but every one who is not by nature God.

Jehovah is the incommunicable name of the true God, denoting his everlasting permanent existence; and God declareth this by calling himself, *I am,* which expresseth the meaning of Jehovah. Now the psalmist affirms that the name *Jehovah* belongs to none but the true God, saying, *Thou, whose name alone is Jehovah, art the most high over all the earth;* yet this name is given unto Christ in the Old Testament. I mention only one place out of many, *This is his name whereby he shall be called the Lord* (in the Hebrew, Jehovah) *our righteousness.*

Jesus takes to himself the incommunicable name, saying, *Before Abraham was, I am;* and thereby intimates to the Jews, that he was the very I AM who spake to Moses at the bush; the God of Abraham, Isaac, and Jacob, who brought the Israelites out of Egypt, gave them his law at Sinai, and led them by his cloud, and fed them with his manna in the wilderness.

Paul tells you that the God, the I AM, who was tempted by the Israelites in the wilderness, was Christ; *neither let us tempt Christ, as some of them also tempted, and were destroyed by serpents.*

John ascribes *eternal existence* unto Christ, saying,

The life was manifested, and we have seen it, and shew unto you that eternal life *which was with the Father, and was manifested unto us.* Well, sir, are you growing weary of this Scripture evidence?

No, no, doctor, you have me fast by the ears. I love Scripture much, but hate your logic, for I have suffered by it. Last Shrove-tide, I was riding to a market, and overtook a very spruce fellow, who quickly let me know he was a philosopher. I can, he said, dispute upon a broomstick for half a day together. I can take any side of any question, and prove it first very right, and then mighty wrong. I can fix an ass so equally between two hay bundles, that though he is hungry, and placed within due reach of both, he shall taste of neither. I offered to lay him half a crown, that the ass would fairly eat both the bundles, if convenient time was granted. No, he replied, the ass will not; and I shall prove that he cannot. Nay, then, said I, it is no common ass, if he will not eat good hay; it must be some human ass like yourself, sir; and so I jogged on and left him. Indeed, these broomstick disputers had almost choused me out of Christ's divinity. Go on, doctor, I am not weary, but am all attention.

Sir, I obey your orders cheerfully; it is a favorite subject, and concerns me much. If Jesus Christ is not truly God, he cannot save me. No atonement can be made by his death. Neither need he come from heaven, merely as a prophet, to instruct me. He might have taught me just the same things by the mouth of Paul or Peter, as by his own mouth; and they might have confirmed the truth by their death, as well as himself. But they could make no atonement on a cross for sin. None but a real God-man can do this. And now, sir, I proceed.

God claims divine worship as due only to himself. *Thou shalt worship the Lord thy God, and him* only *shalt thou serve.* And Paul makes idolatry to consist in paying service or worship to *them that are not gods by nature.* If, therefore, Jesus Christ is not God by *nature,* he ought not to be worshipped. Yet when the Father brought his Son into the world, he said, *Let all the angels of God* worship *him.* And that multitude of heavenly host, which brought the shepherds tidings of a Saviour, no doubt did worship him accordingly.

Many patients that came to Jesus for a cure did *worship* him, and without a reprimand for so doing.

All his disciples *worshipped* him very solemnly at his ascension.

All angels and glorified saints pay him *worship* in heaven, saying, *Worthy is the Lamb that was slain, to receive power, and riches, and wisdom, and strength, and honor, and glory, and blessing!* What a number of words are heaped together, in order to express the highest worship and the deepest adoration! Yet lofty men cannot submit to *worship* Jesus, though the angels do it cheerfully.

Again — *Every creature in heaven, on earth, and under the earth, say, Blessing, and honor, and glory, and power, be to him that sittest on the throne, and to the Lamb, for ever and ever.* Every creature is here represented as paying, and every creature will at length be forced to pay, this homage and worship *equally* to the Father and the Lamb; which yet never would be paid, unless Christ was truly God. For thus the Lord declares, *I am Jehovah, that is my name; and my glory will I not give to another*, that is, to any other who is not Jehovah. But Jesus Christ's name is Jehovah too, and therefore he shares equal glory with the Father.

Jesus, as Jehovah, is the object of prayer. The apostles say, *Lord, increase our faith.*

All petitioners who applied to Christ for help, presented their prayer to him, and expected help wholly from him, excepting Martha, who is gently reproved for not doing so. Martha says, *I know that whatsoever thou wilt ask of God, he will give it thee.* Jesus tells her, *I am the resurrection and the life: he that believeth on me, though he were dead, yet shall he live.* You talk of God's giving me whatsoever I ask; but know assuredly, that I have life in myself, and raise a soul or body unto life, when I please.

Stephen says, *Lord, lay not this sin to their charge;* and commends his departing soul, as true believers do, into the hand of Jesus. And who, but Jehovah, is worthy of, and sufficient for, such a trust?

Paul, in a prayer, puts the Son's name before the Father's — *May our Lord Jesus Christ himself, and God, even our Father, comfort your hearts, and stablish you in every good word and work.*

In the New Testament, Christians are thus described, *They* call upon *the name of Jesus Christ.* This was an outward distinguishing *mark* of Christians in the apostle's day, but some lewd professors in our day esteem it the *brand* of idolaters.

It is the Father's will, *that all should honor the Son,* even as *they honor the Father;* should pay the same adoration and worship to the Son, in his human nature, as they pay it to the Father. The *human nature*, taken by the Son, vailed his divinity; and might seem a bar against divine worship. Therefore a command is given, first, that all the angels should worship him at his incarnation; and then, *that all men should honor the Son*, even as *they honor the Father*. The union of the two natures shall be no bar against divine worship. And every one who withholdeth this honor from the Son, does withhold it from the Father, and dishonor him. For *he that honoreth not the Son, honoreth not the Father, who hath sent him.*

When you direct a prayer unto Jesus, you need no one to introduce you, but may go *directly* to him now, as they did aforetime when he was on earth. As man, he receives the addresses of men; and as God, he is worthy of them, and abundantly able to supply all wants. But when you pray to the Father or the Holy Spirit, that is, to the Godhead absolutely, then you must go through the Mediator, as the only ground of your acceptance.

We are baptized *equally* into the name of the Father and the Son, and thereby make *equal* profession of faith, worship, and obedience to them both. But if Jesus Christ is not Jehovah, raise him up as high as the shoulder of an Arian can lift him, he is still much more beneath the Father than a worm is beneath himself. For there is no proportion between finite and infinite. Therefore if Jesus Christ is not Jehovah, to couple him with the Father in the same baptismal dedication, is a thousand times more unseemly than to harness a snail and an elephant together. And what is said of the Son in this article, equally respects the Holy Ghost.

Jesus Christ is appointed the judge of quick and dead; but how can he execute the office unless he is Jehovah? His eye must survey every moment all the actions, words, and thoughts that are passing everywhere throughout the earth; and his memory must retain distinctly all the amazing number of actions, words, and thoughts, that will have passed from the world's creation till its dissolution. If but a single wickedness, committed in a sinner's bosom, escapes him; or but a single *cup of cold water, given unto any in the name of a disciple*, is forgotten; he cannot judge right judgment. Now, if you think a creature's comprehension can survey and retain all these things — and modern faith, though straining out a Bible-gnat, will swallow down a hundred camels — still I ask, how can Jesus know the hearts of men, unless he is Jehovah? This prerogative belongs to God *alone*.

Solomon prays in this manner, *Jehovah, God of Israel, thou, even thou only, knowest the hearts of all the children of men.* And Jehovah says of himself, *I search the heart, and try the reins.*

Now Jesus does the same; therefore he is Jehovah, and qualified to be a judge. He shewed, while on earth, that *he knew what was in man;* he *knew their thoughts;* disclosed the inward *reasonings of their hearts;* and declares concerning himself, *that all the churches shall know that I am he who search the reins and hearts;* and being able to do this, he is qualified for judge, and therefore adds, *I will give to every one of you, according to your works.*

The divinity of Christ proved a sad bone of contention among the Jews, who judged of him from his mean appearance, and not from his godlike works and words. At one time he tells them, *I and my Father are one.* The Jews understood his meaning well, and cried out, *We stone thee for blasphemy, because that thou, being a man, makest thyself God.*

At another time he says, *My Father worketh hitherto, and I work.* I work with uncontrolled power, as my Father works; and all things obey me and my Father equally. Hereupon the Jews sought to kill him, because he had said that *God was his Father* (ἴδιον πατέρα,) his own proper or *peculiar* Father), *making himself thereby* equal *with God.* The Jews knew, though some among ourselves do not, what Jesus meant by calling God his *own proper* Father. They perceived by this expression, that he made himself so partake of his Father's *divine* nature, as an earthly son partakes of his father's *human* nature, which is the same in both; and that Jesus hereby would distinguish himself both from angels, who are *created* sons of God, and from believers, who are *adopted* sons; and for this expression, which seemed presumptuous and blasphemous, they sought to kill him.

On another occasion, Jesus took the incommunicable name to himself, saying, *before Abraham was,* I AM; and this so enraged the Jews, *that they took up stones to cast at him.* Now stoning was the legal punishment for *blasphemy.*

When Jesus is accused of blasphemy for making himself God, he never does refute the charge, but either vindicates his high claim in a *covert* way, which was needful then, that his death might not be hastened; or he passeth over the charge in silence. And is silence, in such a weighty matter, consistent with the character of Jesus? If he had not been Jehovah, surely it behoves him, when called a blasphemer, to tell them plainly, "You mistake my words, I am not God, nor meant to call myself so."

This charge of blasphemy pursued Jesus through his ministry, and at length nailed him to the cross. At his trial, he is first brought before the Jewish council, where some frivolous things are urged, but nothing proved. Then Caiaphas stands up, and says, *Art thou the* Son *of the blessed?* Christ's appointed hour was now come, and his answer is no longer covert; *Jesus saith,* I AM. The high-priest, knowing well the meaning of his words, *rends his clothes, and says, What need have we of further witnesses. Ye have heard his* blasphemy. *What think ye? And they all condemned him to be guilty of death.*

Next he is hurried before the bar of Pilate, to have their sentence confirmed. Here, again, some idle matters are first urged, but not regarded by the governor. Jesus is accused of aspiring to be king, but satisfies Pilate by declaring, *his kingdom is not of this world.* At length the capital charge of *blasphemy* is brought, which finished the trial. *We have a law, say the Jews, and by our law he ought to die, because he made himself the* SON *of God. Pilate, hearing this, was much* afraid; *and going to the judgment-hall* again, *says to Jesus, Whence art thou? But Jesus gave him no answer. Pilate saith, Speakest thou not unto me? Knowest thou not that I have power to crucify thee, and power to release thee? Jesus answered, Thou couldest have no power at all against me, except it were given thee from above: therefore he that delivered me unto thee, hath the greater sin.* This answer somewhat checked Pilate, but an outcry from the Jews quickens him, and he passeth sentence.

Thus both at the bar of Caiaphas and Pilate, the capital charge brought against Jesus was blasphemy, or the calling himself in a peculiar sense the Son of God, and thereby making himself *equal* with God. For this he was condemned to die; and he suffered death as a blasphemer for laying claim to divinity. And were he now in Britain, a multitude of those who are fed at his altar would lift a heel against him, and hail him to a gibbet, and cry out as before, *If thou be the* SON *of God, come down* from thy gallows, *and we will believe* that thou art the proper Son of God—neither an *adopted* Son, nor a *created* Son, but *the only begotten Son of the Father.*

Perhaps they might go further—so great is their zeal—and having crucified the Saviour on a false charge of blasphemy, might crucify his followers on a base pretence of idolatry. A minute philosopher has *dared* to publish muttering words about it; one who likes to live upon the alms arising from the Lord's service, and can say genteelly, *Hail, Master*, and betray the Master's honor as a friend of old did.

When Jesus says, *the Father is greater than he*, and the Son is ignorant of the day of judgment, these things must be ascribed to his human nature. As touching his Godhead, he is equal to the Father, being declared to be *one* with the Father, one in nature, and bearing his *express image;* but as touching his manhood, is inferior to the Father: and his human nature, we are told *grew in wisdom and stature*, which supposeth a finite boundary.

And though at last the kingdom of Christ will be delivered up to the Father, this must be understood of his mediatorial kingdom. All things are administered at present by the hand of Jesus, as God-man mediator; but when this dispensation ends, the kingdom will return to its original order; and, when thus returned, it is not said the *Father* will be all in all, but *God* (the triune God) will be all in all.

That the Son will not lose his *essential* kingdom as God, when his *mediatorial* kingdom as God-man ceaseth, seems plain from these words of the Father to the Son— *Thy throne, O God, is for ever and ever;* which words ascribe an *everlasting* dominion to the Son, when his mediatorial kingdom is no more.

Thus, Sir, I have given you a summary proof of Christ's divinity from the Bible; and can you suppose that the Scripture would tell you plainly, again and again, that Jesus Christ is *Jehovah — is God*—the *true God* — the *mighty God*—the *just God*—and *God over all, blessed for evermore*, if he was not truly God? All these lofty expressions are applied to Jesus Christ, and they would naturally mislead plain men, yea, and would confound all plain language, if he is not truly God. A man must have the old serpent's subtlety, and chop and mince his logic mighty fine, who can banish Christ's divinity out of these expressions. But what, then, must become of the poor, who are the chief subjects of the gospel-kingdom? They cannot buy the spawn of subtle brains, nor, if purchased, could digest it. They have nothing but the Bible, and if Jesus is not truly God, the Bible would mislead them; and so, for want of a scribe's cap and dictionary, they must all miscarry truly.

You have heard before, that *the wise are taken in their own craftiness;* and now, sir, hear how the Lord *takes* them. Gins and snares are scattered in his word to catch a subtle scribe, just as traps are laid by us to catch a fox or foulmart. Every fundamental doctrine meets with something which *seems* directly to oppose it; and these *seeming* contradictions are the traps which are laid. A lofty scribe, who depends upon his own subtlety, and cannot pray sincerely for direction, is sure to be taken in these snares; but a humble praying soul escapes them, or, if his foot be caught, the snare is broken, and his soul delivered.

Some things spoken of the *human nature* of Christ, and of his *mediatorial* character and office, are the traps laid about his divinity to catch a modern scribe; as the meanness of Christ's appearance in Judea was a trap to catch an ancient rabbi.

Isaiah has an awful word about these traps which are laid around the Saviour's person. *He* (Jesus) *shall be for a sanctuary* (unto some), *but for a stone of stumbling and a rock of offence to both the houses of Israel; for a* gin *and for a* snare *to the inhabitants of Jerusalem.* And they were taken in the *snare*, for they crucified the *Lord of glory* as a vile blasphemer.

No one has cause to complain of these traps, because the Holy Spirit's guidance is promised to all them that seek it earnestly; and if men are too lazy or too lofty to seek this assistance, they are justly suffered to *stumble, and fall, and be broken, and be* snared, *and be taken.*

But, sir, if you would take a modern rabbi for your tutor, and seat yourself beneath his feet, and catch the droppings of his mouth, whither, whither must you fly for shelter? Alas! the modern scribes are just in such a hobble now about Jesus, as the Jewish scribes were. Some said then, *he is John the baptist;* others said, No; *he is Elias;* and others contradicted both, and called him *Jeremias, or one of the prophets.* So it was then; and so it is now. Some say, he is a *mere man,* as the Turks say; and such professors only need a pair of whiskers, to pass for Mussulmen. Others say, he has an *angel's nature,* but is head and shoulders taller than the highest angel; others contradict them both, and say, he is *a* God; but having lost a small article in St. John's Greek gospel, he is not *the* God. Others laugh at this, and say, he is no God at all, but hoisted into Godship by his office; and must be worshipped in a lower strain, as wily courtiers worship princes, as starving Levites worship patrons, as antiquarians worship rust, or as Christian men will worship mammon.

Again, whilst some affirm he is not truly God, others have affirmed he was not truly man, or had no real human nature; and so amongst them all they have stripped him worse than the Roman soldiers did, who took his clothes, yet left his carcass; but these rogues have run away with every thing. According to their various fancies, he is neither God, nor angel, nor man; and what else they can make him, I see not, unless it be a devil, as the Jewish scribes made him.

Thus Jesus proves a sad *stone of stumbling* to the lofty scribes who flounder round about him, and bedaub him grievously, but cannot get up to him; and as every scribe grows sharper than his brother, some new nature is invented for the Saviour. And, sir, if you renounce the plain account of the Bible, you will find as many caps for Christ's head, as there are fancies in a scribe's brain.

If Jesus Christ is not truly God, all his apostles, excepting Judas, were idolaters; for they *worshipped* him with great solemnity at his ascension. Also all the Christians of the first and purest age were idolaters; for we learn from undoubted heathen records, that they prayed and sang praises to *one Jesus*, according to the character given them by Paul, *They call upon the name of Jesus Christ our Lord in every place.* Yea, and all the angels too, except the devils, are highly guilty of idolatry; for they sing delightful praises unto God and the Lamb. Which adoration puts the devils, who are utter haters of idolatry, in a cruel rage at the book of Revelations, where this worship is recorded, and makes them raise up human tools to vilify the book, and try to banish it from the sacred canon.

Enough, enough, doctor; put no more sheaves upon the cart, lest you break it down. An overstocked market oversets it commonly; and a drove of lean proofs coming after the other, may prove like Pharaoh's second drove of lean oxen, which devoured all the fat ones. I would have no more than just enough — cramming only breeds a surfeit. And I have heard enough to satisfy me that Jesus is my Maker and Preserver — the God in whom I live, and move, and have my being — who deserves my highest worship and my best obedience. And it seems agreeable to common sense, that none can *redeem* a world but the *Maker* of it. Yet I am still in the dark about your new covenant. How does it differ from the old;

and how must I get a slice of the new? Nature, you say, cannot carve for herself; who, then, must do this office for her, and put the meat upon her trencher?

An answer to both your questions will occasion some little repetition, sir, yet not a needless one, since it respects the *way* to life, which is too commonly mistaken.

In a covenant of works, a man must work for life by his *own will* and *power*, or by the natural abilities he is endowed with. He stands upon his own legs, and had need look well to them; for the tenor of this covenant is, *Do, and live; transgress, and die.* A single trip ruins all; as in angels, so in Adam; but if the whole is kept without a flaw, a right to life is purchased by virtue of the covenant *promise.*

In the covenant of grace, all things are *purchased* for us, and *bestowed* upon us, *graciously* or freely.

These two covenants are called the old and new; no more are noticed in Scripture; and a suitable *law* respecting both is mentioned—*the law of works, and the law of faith.* All other laws are cobwebs of a human brain—such as the law of *sincere obedience,* the law of *love,* &c. For love and obedience are the *fruits* of faith, and not the *law* of the new covenant.

And now, sir, God himself shall tell you by the mouth of Jeremiah what the new covenant is. *Behold, the days come, saith the Lord, that* I *will make a new* covenant *with the house of Israel,* not like *that I made at Sinai; but this shall be the covenant,* I will *put my law in their inward parts, and write it in their hearts;* I will *be their God, and they* shall *be my people;* I will *forgive their iniquities, and remember their sins no more.*

Ezekiel describes this covenant more minutely — *I will sprinkle clean water upon you, and ye shall be clean; I will cleanse you from all your filthiness and all your idols; I will give you a new heart, and I will put a* new *spirit in you; I will take the stony heart out of your flesh, and I will give you an heart of flesh; I will put* my Spirit *within you, and* cause *you to walk in my statutes.*

The *new* covenant is here shown to consist of a rich and gracious bundle of free promises, in which *I will* and *I will* runs through the whole. God does not say, "Make yourselves obedient, and then I will sprinkle clean water upon you, to wash away guilt;" but he says, "*I will* do both; I will pardon you, and make you obedient also; yea, *I will* do everything, and do it by *my Spirit.* Not your own might, but *my Spirit* shall sanctify your heart, and engage your feet to walk in my statutes."

This covenant is too glorious for nature to behold. She shrinks from the dazzling sight; fears woful consequences from it; and, trembling for morality, beseeches the vicar to marry Moses unto Jesus, and couple the two covenants. From this adulterous alliance springs the spurious covenant of faith and works, with a spruce new set of duties, half a yard long, called legally-evangelical, or evangelically-legal; unknown to Christ and his apostles, but discovered lately by some ingenious gentlemen.

However, Jesus does not thank old nature for her fears. He has promised in his covenant to provide a new heart, and good feet, as well as justification and pardon; and what he promiseth he will perform. Jesus does not want the staff of Moses; nor will the master of the house suffer an alliance with his servant.

And so much, sir, for the nature of the new covenant. Your next question was — How do we become partakers of it? Now the blessings of this covenant were all purchased by Jesus, and are lodged in his hand to dispose of; free pardons to bless a guilty sinner, free grace to sanctify his nature, with full power to lead him safe to Canaan. Jesus therefore says, *Look to me and be saved; Come to me and I will give you rest.* But the bare command and invitation of his Word will not bring us to him.

Nature lost her legs in paradise, and has not found them since; nor has she any *will* to come to Jesus. The way is steep and narrow, full of self-denials, crowded up with stumbling-blocks. She cannot like it; and, when she does come, it is with huge complaining. Moses is obliged to flog her tightly, and make her heart ache, before she will cast a weeping look on Jesus. Once she doated on this Jewish lawgiver, was fairly wedded to him, and sought to please him by her *works*, and he seemed a kindly husband; but now he grows so fierce a tyrant, there is no bearing of him. When she takes a wry step, his mouth is always full of cursing; and his resentments are so implacable, no weeping will appease him, nor promise of amendment.

Why, doctor, you are got into your altitudes — I do not understand you. Figures are above my match; I never could get through arithmetic. Pray, let us have plain English.

So you shall, sir. Man is born under the law of works, and of course is wedded to that law; it is the law of his nature. Traces of the moral law are still upon his heart; the fall has blotted the two tables, but not defaced them wholly. Where revelation is bestowed, the tables are renewed as at Sinai; but only wrote as yet in stone, not on the heart. By means of the moral sense and revelation, men acquire some notion of a covenant of works. This covenant suits their nature, and is understood in a measure, though neither in its full extent, nor in its awful penalties. Jesus begins his lectures with the *law of works*, somewhat known to the scholar, and urges that law on his conscience with vigor, to drive him to the *law of faith*. The young Israelite is called to Mount Sinai, where Jesus trains his people now, as he did aforetime. And till the heart has had a thorough schooling here, has heard and felt the thunders of the law, it will be hard and stony. It may be pitiful to others, but wants compassion for itself; may weep at a neighbor's ruin, but cannot truly feel for its own. The bosom is so bound about with wrappers of obedience, that when the curses of the law are heard, they only tingle in the ear, and graze upon the breast, but do not pierce the conscience. The man knoweth not his real danger; the law of works refreshes him; and while he sippeth comfort from his faint obedience, Jesus Christ is only used as a make-weight — like the small dust thrown in a scale to turn the balance.

Now Sinai breaks the legal heart, and takes the stone away. Here the *heart of flesh* is given; Jesus, by his Spirit, sets the law home upon the sinner's conscience; then he *feels* that the curses in the law are his proper portion — not because he is the chief of sinners, but because he is a sinner. Thus his bosom is unswaddled, the heart begins to bleed, the mouth is stopped quite, all legal worthiness is gone, he stands condemned by the law, and *all* his hope is fixed on Jesus. While the law was written only upon paper, he found no galling condemnation. His heart, like the stony tables, received the letter, and felt no impression; but when the commandment reached his inmost soul, then he died. This makes a *free* salvation highly needful, a *whole* Saviour truly precious, and a *pure* covenant of grace delightful. And now the scholar comes to Jesus Christ with cap in hand, and bended knee, and bleeding heart, and with Peter's prayer, *Lord, save, or I perish.*

Being thus convinced of sin, his heart can have no rest till he *receives* a pardon, and finds that peace of God *which passeth understanding.* He feels a real condemnation, and must have absolution, not from man, but God. Once he prayed for pardon, and rose up from his knees contentedly without it. His heart was whole, he did not want a pardon; nay, it seemed a presumption to expect it. Yet sure, what we may *ask* without presumption, we may *expect* without presumption. But now the scholar sees his legal title unto heaven is lost, and finds a legal condemnation in his breast besides, which makes him hasten to the *surety*, and call upon him, *as the Lamb of God who takes away our sins*, and as *the Lord our righteousness.* He views the surety, as his law-fulfiller, both as his *legal title*, and his *legal sacrifice;* and he wants an application of these blessings to his heart — an application by the Holy Spirit, to witness they are placed to his account.

He sees a need that both the *legal title* and the *legal sacrifice* should be imputed to answer all the law's demands. And he marvels much that any who allow the imputation of Christ's *death* should yet object to the imputation of his *life*. Since, if the obedience of Christ's death may be *imputed*, or placed to our account, for pardon, why may not the obedience of his life be *imputed* also for justification, or a title unto glory? One is fully as easy to conceive of as the other. Both are purchased by the surety; both are wanted to discharge our legal debts; and both will be embraced and sought with eagerness, when our debts and wants are truly known. But here the matter sticks: men do not feel their wants, and so reject *imputed* righteousness. The heart must be broken down, and humbled well, before it can *submit to this righteousness.* Till we see ourselves utter bankrupts, we shall *go about to establish our own righteousness*, and cannot rest upon the surety's obedience, the God-man's righteousness, as our legal title unto glory.

But, sir, this is not all. Every one who is born of God is made to hunger for *implanted* holiness, as well as thirst for *imputed* righteousness. They want a *meetness* for glory, as well as *title* to it; and know they could not bear to live with God, unless renewed in his image. Heaven would not suit them without holiness, nor could they see the face of God without it. And having felt the *guilt* of sin, and the *plague* of their sinful nature, by *conviction from the Holy Spirit*, this has taught them both to dread sin and loathe it — to *loathe* it for its vile uncleanness, and dread it for the curse it brings. They consider sin as bringing both the devil's nature and the devil's hell. They view it and detest it, as the poison of the moral world, the filthiness of a spirit, the loathing of a Holy God, and such a cursed abomination, as nothing but the blood of Christ could purge away.

And, sir, where *imputed righteousness* is not only *credited* as a gospel doctrine, but *received* by the Holy Spirit's application, it produces love to Jesus — tender love, with gratitude. And this divine love not only makes us willing to *obey* him, but makes us *like* him: for *God* is *love.*

Christian holiness, springing from the application of imputed righteousness, is a glorious work indeed — far exceeding moral decency, its thin shadow, and its dusky image. It is a true devotedness of heart to God, a seeking of his glory, walking in his fear and love, rejoicing in him as a reconciled Father, and delighted with his service, as the only freedom.

Full provision is made for this holiness in the new covenant; and Jesus, the noble king of Israel, bestows it on his subjects. Let me repeat his words, *I will give a new heart, and put my Spirit within you, and cause you to walk in my statutes.* Believers look to him with prayer and faith; by looking are *transformed into his image;* and taste the blessed fruits of Canaan before they pass the banks of Jordan.

But, sir, the holiest Christian can put *no* trust in his holiness. His daily seeking to *grow in grace*, proves his holiness defective. *Tekel* is written on every duty, *Thou art weighed in the balance and found wanting.* And he knows the meaning of those weighty words, applicable both to soul and body — *Verily, every man at his* best estate, *is* altogether *vanity.* His utmost holiness and freest services do not answer the demand of God's law; and if depended on for justification in *any* measure, would bring him under the law's penalty, and condemn him. He is therefore forced to fly out of himself *entirely*, and seek a refuge *only* in Christ.

Nay, doctor, you must not take your gloves out yet, nor handle your staff, as if preparing for a march. I have a bag of foxes by my side, which must be let out, one by one, before we part. If you can hunt them down, it will be well; if not, they may spoil your sheepfold, and worry all your doctrine.

Sir, I am sick of foxes. My father gave me one, and I am bound to keep him during life. Every day I smell him, and scarce know how to keep him chained in his kennel, he is so crafty. His kennel and your bag, I suppose, are just the same, nothing but a human breast. And sure no fox is half so full of wiles, as the human heart.

Well, but doctor, I must open my bag. Pray, take a peep on this young cub, and listen to his chatter. "Faith!" he cries, "what is faith? Every simpleton who has learnt his creed may believe, though he cannot reckon twenty. Pooh! I would not give a straw for all the faith of all your ancient and your modern saints — not I; give me a budget of good works. Faith! what can faith do? A poor empty thing without a grain of *merit.* The other night I waited on friend *Sarle*, your honest neighbor, and supped in his henroost, amidst a deal of cackling music. When I marched off, a straggling goose was hard at hand, and I was much inclined to ask her to my lodging; for company is pleasant, and the night was dark: but my stomach being crammed with poultry, and a barking dog appearing, I let the waddling dame go off quietly. This noble act of mercy, such as Christians often shew, must justify me more than a thousand of your piteous acts of faith." You hear doctor, how he chatters.

Yes, sir, so I could chatter once; and we are apt to undervalue what we do not understand. But all possessors of divine faith esteem it highly, and call it, as St. Peter does, *precious faith*. It brings a *precious* view of Christ, and draweth *precious* blessings from him. It is a grace which quarrels much with human pride, and makes its only boast of Jesus; and is not meant to be our *justifying* righteousness, else it might learn to boast too. Faith says, *In the Lord have I righteousness;* and tells a sinner, "I cannot save thee:" *Thou art saved by grace through faith*. The *grace* of Jesus brings salvation; and *through faith*, as an instrument put in the sinner's hand, he is enabled to reach the grace; just as a beggar, by his empty cap stretched forth, receives an alms.

A pole held to a drowning man, and by which he is drawn to land, saveth him, just as faith saves a sinner. In a lax way of speaking, we are said to be saved by faith; and so the drowning man might say he was saved by the pole, though in truth he was rescued by the mercy of a neighbor, who thrust a pole towards him, and thereby drew him safe on shore.

Faith could have no room in a covenant of grace, if it had any *justifying* righteousness of its own. For desert on man's part is not consistent with such a covenant: *Else grace is no longer grace.*

If any personal or relative duty, such as temperance or charity, had been made the instrument of obtaining gospel-blessings, we might fancy some peculiar worth was in that duty to procure the blessings. But when faith, which is only lifting up an empty hand or a longing eye to Jesus, is made the instrument of salvation, it is clearly shewn that the covenant is of grace wholly, both in its contrivance and conveyance. *It is* therefore *of faith, that it might be by grace.*

God has chosen this foolish instrument as the means of receiving salvation, *that no flesh might glory in his presence.* Yet foolish as the instrument may seem, it is of curious heavenly workmanship. No man, with all his wit, can make it; though many act the ape, and mimic it. *This foolishness of God is wiser than men:* they cannot comprehend it; but growl at God as dogs howl at the moon.

Doctor, I must open my bag again: young cubs, I find, are not regarded by you. Pray, cast a look upon this old fox; see what a marvellous length of grizzly beard he has got! Sure he must have been as old as Cain, and hunted oft by Enoch. He bears a very *decent* countenance, you see; and though a secret thief all his days, will preach about good works, I warrant him, and hope to make a penny of them; but hear him.

"None can justly claim more merit than a fox. He nightly watches every neighbor's fold and henroost; and, like an upright justice, takes up every vagrant that he meets. Yet notwithstanding all our vigilance, we are often vilified as evil-doers, and are told by the bawling methodists, that our good works will not justify us. Faith, you know, is not a fox's traffic: our commerce lies in works, and by good works we live. Yet some have lately laid us on so thick with texts of faith, that we were gravelled by them, till an ancient Reynard started up and said, why, sure the Bible can afford more justifications than one. This proved a lucky thought, and was happily pursued. One fox started a brace presently, another sprung a leash, and a third found two brace sitting. You may think our hearts were much refreshed by these reports, and the justifications were in this order; first by faith alone, then by works alone, then by faith and works conjointly, and then by neither faith nor works at all. We are pretty sure of escaping by one or another of these methods, and are determined to try them all round. In the meantime, we have fixed on works for the first hearing, because the doctors tells us that only faith can justify us upon earth; but they add, though *works* cannot justify us here below, they may chance to justify us in the world above. For, say they, who can tell what the next world is, and whether heavenly beings think so highly of good works as foxes do? Cain, Ahitophel, and Judas, one in each dispensation, are retained as our counsel, who have promised to exert their utmost. And we do not doubt it, because they have been cast in the first trial, for want of faith; and their next chance lieth, like ours, in the merit of their works." Well, doctor, you have heard this subtle orator; what think you?

I think, sir, if he gets a testimonial, the fox may turn a Levite. His creed might suit a modern pulpit, and a sheepfold would suit him; it affords good picking. But to the business. The *obedience* of Christ, our surety, is the ground and *meritorious* cause of justification. Paul asserts, *We are justified* freely *by grace through the redemption that is in Christ Jesus.* He declares roundly, *By the obedience of* ONE, even Christ, *shall many be made righteous;* and affirms that *the righteousness of God* (the God-man surety), *is unto all, and upon all, that believe;* is imputed *unto* all that believe; and put *upon* all, as their justification robe. David will *make mention of this righteousness, and of this only.* Isaiah tells you what the church's faith was in his day, *surely* in *the Lord have I righteousness;* and Peter writes to them, *who have obtained precious faith,* not through, but in *the righteousness of our* God and Saviour Jesus Christ.

On the other hand, Paul declares, *By the deeds of the law, no flesh living shall be justified in God's sight;* and intimates that a justification by works would destroy the covenant of grace, *To him that worketh, the reward is not reckoned of* grace, *but of* debt; that is, if any could justify himself by works, his reward would be a *legal debt,* and not the *gift* of *gospel grace.* The text alone, if there was no other, would exclude all justification by works, as inconsistent with a covenant of grace. For if we are justified *wholly* by works, the reward would be *wholly* of debt; if justified in *part,* it would be *partly* of debt. But God has no *debts* to pay in the gospel. *It is the* grace *of God which brings salvation,* and *no flesh shall glory in his presence.*

Thus the Bible declares that no man shall be justified *before* God by his works; that men are justified by faith; and that faith only justifies by resting on the obedience of Christ as the *meritorious* cause of justification.

But this matter may require some enlargement. The Scripture comprehends all wicked men in the general name of unbelievers; and Jesus says, *He that believeth not is condemned* already. How is that? Why, every man is a sinner; and the law declares, *the wages of sin is death.* Of course a sentence of death is passed on every sinner, and if he dies in unbelief, he needs no *second* condemnation, because he is condemned *already.* But the sentence of the law is a *silent* verdict, not heard and felt by unconvinced sinners, else they would fly to Jesus; neither does the law declare the various measures of that death, which are due to various sinners; it only says in general, "Cursed are you, and ye shall die."

Hence we may learn what is the judge's office at the grand assize, not to pass a *second* condemnation on the wicked — that would be needless, they are condemned *already* — but to make an *open declaration* of that secret verdict which the law has passed, and then appoint the various measures of that death which are due to sinners.

When a jury, in our courts of justice, find a culprit guilty, the judge passeth sentence. But is the judge's sentence a *second* condemnation? Not at all. The jury do condemn the culprit, and the judge *pronounceth* sentence according to the jury's verdict, and then declares the punishment to be inflicted on the convict.

A sinner therefore is not first condemned on earth for want of faith, and then condemned in the clouds a *second* time for want of righteousness. No; his *state* of misery is finally determined by unbelief — *He that believeth not shall be damned;* but the *measure* of his misery depends upon the measure of his own iniquity. Unbelief *alone* condemns the sinner; and in consequence of that condemnation, he suffers punishment according to his crimes.

We may now consider how it fareth with believers. Jesus saith, *Whosoever believeth in the Son of man, shall not perish, but have eternal life.* And it is further said, *He that believeth on the Son hath*, or possesseth, everlasting *life.* Here we read that faith gives a *present* possession of *everlasting* life. It is begun in the soul on earth, and shall be perfected in heaven; and to strengthen the believer's hope, it is added, *he shall not perish.* A full absolution from eternal misery, and a full promise of eternal life, with a *present* possession of it, is granted to believers on the mere account of faith. And what security can they further want or have?

Again, it is said, *All that believe are justified from all things.* Now I ask, if believers are justified *already*, what further justification can they *need?* And if justified from *all things*, what further justification can they *have?* It is not possible to be more justified than from *all things*, and so far believers are justified in the present life.

The Scripture speaketh of a *first* and *second* covenant, but nowhere speaketh of a *first* and *second* justification. Such a twofold justification must suppose there are degrees in it, and that the latter increaseth the former, else it is needless: but this is quite repugnant to its nature. For justification is an individual whole, like a unit. Take anything from a unit, or add anything to it, and it ceaseth to be a unit. So the man who is truly justified is justified from *all things;* and such a one cannot possibly be *more* justified, nor can be *less* than justified.

Beloved John might have more of Christ's affection than Philip, and a brighter crown than Philip, but could not have more justification than Philip. Because, though there are degrees in the affection and rewards of Christ, there can be no degrees in his justification. A man must either have the whole or none at all; must either be justified from all things, or be condemned.

And now, sir, the justification, which has passed *secretly* in a believer's breast, known indeed to him and declared, but derided by the world, this will be notified publicly by the judge at last, and degrees of glory be assigned to each, according to their various fruitfulness.

Thus a believer's *state* of happiness is finally determined by his faith: *He that believeth shall be saved;* but the *measure* of his happiness in that state depends upon the *fruits* of faith. Faith *alone* saves a Christian; but his crown is brighter according as his faith works more abundantly by love.

But another matter must be taken into this account, beside the declaration of the proper sentences, and assignment of the proper retributions. David says, *the Lord will be justified when he speaketh; and be cleared when he judgeth.* The world neither know nor regard the faith, *which is of God's operation,* but are content with one of human manufacture; and finding no advantage from this faith, they consider all faith as a trifling or a despicable matter. It appeareth such an idle business as can never justify, and seemeth such a reflection upon God, to assign that office to it; yea, and all that wear the gospel-cloak of faith, full and deep, are thought enthusiasts or impostors, men who have lost their wits, or lost their honesty, and fit only for Bedlam or for Newgate.

Now when Jesus judgeth, he will *clear* this matter up, and vindicate the credit and appointment of faith. He will show what fruits have been produced by faith; and though they cannot justify the little flock before God, yet when openly proclaimed by the judge, they will *justify* him in the choice of the instrument, and will *justify* believers evermore from all aspersions cast upon them by the world, as if they were not zealous of good works, because they renounced all dependence on them.

Take notice, sir, how the judge speaks to the sheep on his right hand. A choice fruit of faith, the sanctification of the heart, our *meetness* for glory, is not even mentioned by him; because the world could be no witness of it: he only noticeth their *works*, and only such of these as must be public and notorious. *I was hungry, and ye fed me; naked, and ye clothed me; a stranger, and ye took me in; sick or in prison, and ye visited me.* And what say the sheep to this honorable mention? Do they speak, as if expecting to be justified by their works? No: just the contrary. All think themselves such *unprofitable servants*, that they will not own a good work has been done by them. "Lord," say they, "when did we so, or so, as thou hast spoken?"

Jesus next applies himself to the goats on his left, and takes no kind of notice of their *unholy hearts;* for, being strangers to the nature of holiness, they would have cried out, "Lord, we always had *good hearts* — much sounder than those sheep upon your right, who were evermore complaining of their *loathsome* hearts." Jesus therefore directs his speech to their *morality*, and only maketh mention of good works, which they had some knowledge of, and expected to be justified by them. Here he shows they have been wanting, and confounds them in their own hope. Thus the *judge clears himself, when he judgeth;*

The sheep were *justified by* faith; and that act is vindicated to the world by the precious *fruits* of faith. The goats were condemned through *unbelief*, and are silenced by that *unrighteousness* which unbelief produced.

It is observable that not a single sheep expects to be justified by works; yet the goats do expect it, every one. When Jesus tells them, *I was hungry, and ye fed me* not; *naked, and ye clothed me* not; *sick, and ye visited me* not, &c., they answer briskly, *When saw we thee an hungered, or athirst, or naked, or sick, or in prison, and did not minister unto thee?* That is, when were we wanting in our service to thee? Thus they come with a full justification in their mouths, ready for the trial; yet are all confounded.

It is further observable, that Jesus does not charge the goats with never having done *any* acts of charity. No: some of them might have founded schools or colleges; and some have given largely to the Lock and Magdalen, or to assembly-rooms and playhouses: and some might have undone themselves by largesses before or at elections. But when a goat is bountiful, he seeks to please his own humor, or glorify his own name, or promote a distant interest. No true regard is had to Jesus, nor to his little flock; these are always overlooked. The doctrines of the sheep are loathsome, and their bleating trade of prayer is nauseous to a goat. He could wish the world well eased of them all. Therefore Jesus says, Whatever bounty ye have done, *inasmuch as ye did it not to the least of* these my brethren, *ye did it not to me;* in neglecting and despising my own family, ye have neglected and despised me. Therefore, "Depart, ye cursed."

Give me leave to twist another thread about a lash you had before. If the glories of the next world are called *rewards,* they are affirmed to be rewards, not of *debt,* but *of grace;* not due for our works, but bestowed through the grace of Jesus. Eternal death, in all its various horrors, is the just deserved *wages of sin;* but eternal life, in all its various glories, *is the* gift *of God, through Jesus Christ our Lord.* And therefore, though the little flock may be rewarded *according* to their works, they cannot be rewarded for the *merit* of them. A man of plain sense may see a difference here with his naked eye, which yet is often not discerned by a scribe with his microscope.

Take an illustration. A tender-hearted gentleman employs two laborers out of charity, to weed a little spot of four square yards. Both are old and much decrepit, but one is stronger than the other. The stronger weeds three yards, and receives three crowns: the weaker weedeth one, and receives one crown. Now both the laborers are rewarded *for* their labor, and *according to* their labor, but not for the *merit* of their labor. You cannot say their work *deserves* their wages. And yet their work deserves their wages better, an hundred thousand fold, than our poor works can merit an eternal weight of glory.

Oh, sir, God must abominate the pride, the insolence of human pride, which could dream of merit; it is enough to make a devil blush. Yea, and some would purchase heavenly mansions with such scraps of alms as would not buy an earthly toy.

What comes from God is *gift,* and much he has to *give* but nothing that he *sells* for work which we can do. He disdains such paltry commerce, and the saucy tribe of merit-mongers, who can fancy God will *sell* his heaven, and that their works may *purchase* it.

Sir, remember traps are laid around every fundamental doctrine; and I perceive your lips are heaving an objection to the present doctrine. Poor John, disguised in the beard of Moses, and loaded with the Sinai tables, is suborned to betray his master, and *compelled* thus to speak — *Blessed are they that do his commandments, that they may have* right *to the tree of life.* But, sir, if rewards are not of *debt*, as Paul affirms, they are not *due* for our works; and if not *due*, our works have *no right* to the rewards, *no right* to the tree of life; neither does St. John assert it. A mask is put upon his face to hide his look and meaning.

The word which we translate a *right*, signifieth here, as frequently elsewhere, a *gracious privilege*. Thus in his gospel, John says, *As many as received Christ,* that is, *believed on him, to them he gave* (ἐξουσιαν) *the privilege* (as you read it in the Bible margin) *to become the sons of God;* a privilege, not claimed as a *right*, through the *merit* of faith, but bestowed freely, as a *gift*. *To them he* gave *the privilege to become the sons of God.*

Jesus says — *He that believeth possesseth* everlasting *life.* Then by *believing* he must surely enter the city gates, and taste of the tree of life. For if a believer should miscarry, the life he possesseth proveth not an *everlasting* life, but temporary; and the word of Christ falls to the ground.

But a general answer may be given to all objections of this kind. St. John says, *They that do his command-*

ments have a privilege to the tree of life. If you ask what is meant by *doing* his commandments, I answer in one word, *believing.* Nay, sir, do not start like a young colt, but hear and judge like a man. *Working* for life is the law of Moses; *believing* for life is the law of Jesus. And where divine faith is truly found, it will effectually justify, really sanctify, and surely glorify; will bring a sinner out of Egypt, through the wilderness, into Canaan, and fairly perch him on the tree of life.

Hear St. Paul's account of faith, a choice apostle, but no great favorite of the scribes. Human telescopes do not *magnify* Paul; he is not within the compass of their glasses; no moonlight planet, but a star; and take the matter in his own words: — *Made* wise *to salvation by faith* — *become* children *of God by faith* — justified *by faith* — *receive* forgiveness *of sins by faith* — sanctified *by faith* — *receive the* Spirit *through faith* — access *to God by faith* — *Christ* dwelling *in the heart by faith* — work *righteousness through faith* — *obtain* promises *by faith* — walk *by faith* — stand *by faith* — saved *by grace through faith.* And St. Peter adds, *kept by the power of God through faith unto salvation.*

Thus the Christian *life* is a *life of faith in the Son of God;* and the Christian *work* is to *fight this good fight.* Believing is the Christian's trade and maintenance, procures him pardon and holiness, creates his present peace and future prospects, makes him steady and valiant in fight, and brings him triumphantly to glory.

And now, sir, when you hear the Philippian jailor asking Paul *What he must* DO *to be saved*, you need not think the answer was defective, *Believe in the Lord Jesus*

Christ, and thou shalt be saved. This answer of Paul is transcribed from his master's copy, *Go ye into all nations, and preach the gospel to every creature. He that believeth and is baptized shall be saved.* But if Paul's answer was not defective, it is plain, that as *doing* was the sum of the law, so *believing* is the sum of the gospel. It is the *total life* of all duty, and the *total term* of all salvation — including and producing all obedience, yet crucifying all merit. Faith owes its birth, and growth, and blessings, all to Jesus; and it resteth wholly on him, renouncing self, and glorying in the Saviour, as the all in all.

However, since professors frequently amuse themselves with fancies instead of faith, and think a mere assenting unto Scripture doctrines is believing in Christ Jesus, something is often joined with faith to prevent deception. Thus Paul, *In Jesus Christ nothing avails but faith, which worketh by love.* The words, *worketh by love,* are added as the genuine fruit and evidence of faith. If works of love are not produced, the faith is not of God; yet, when produced, they do not justify.

Perhaps you might be pleased to know St. John's thoughts about *keeping the commandments,* because the text was quoted from him; and his mind is intimated in his first epistle, *Whatsoever we ask we receive of him, because we keep his commandments;* and this is his commandment, *that we should believe on the name of his Son Jesus Christ, and love one another.* Does not the latter clause declare that believing on Jesus is *keeping the commandments?* Love indeed is added here, as before by Paul, yet only as an evidence of faith, and a guard against delusion.

Jesus Christ explained the moral law, for the *conviction* of sinners, and for a *rule* of life to believers; but when he declares the *terms* of salvation, nothing is mentioned but *faith*. It is never said *He that believeth* and obeyeth the law *shall be saved*, but absolutely, *he that believeth shall be saved.* Here obedience is designedly kept from our eyes, and withdrawn from faith, to prevent our resting on obedience as a *condition* of salvation, or a *ground* of *justification*.

The apostles also give many rules to direct the walk of faith, and often couple faith with love or obedience, and declare that the faith which produceth not good works, is a dead faith—the cold product of a human brain, and cannot justify. If faith is *alone*, unattended with works, it is not the faith of God, and does not unite the soul to Christ, and cannot draw life from him. But when the apostles speak expressly of justification, you hear of nothing else but faith; then it is *justified by faith—saved by grace through faith—believe in the Lord Jesus, and thou shalt be saved.* At such times, like their master, they purposely drop obedience, to prevent a reliance on it for justification.

When Paul is largely handling the point of justification, he quotes a passage from the Psalms, and introduceth it with this preface, "Even as David describeth the blessedness of the man, unto whom God *imputeth* righteousness *without* works, saying," *Blessed are they, whose iniquities are forgiven, and whose sins are covered, blessed is the man, to whom the Lord will not* impute *sin*. Here Paul breaks off the quotation, and omits the latter clause of the verse, *in whose spirit there is no guile.* And why does he omit the latter clause? Because it describes the *renewed nature* and the *fruit* of a justified person, which were not to be considered in the matter of justification, but wholly withdrawn from our eyes.

We are not justified *before God,* because our natures are renewed; but God *justifies the ungodly through believing.* A sinner can be saved no other way, because the *wages of sin is death;* yet it proves a most offensive way through the pride of a sinner's heart.

Effectual and final justification by faith is the capital doctrine of the Gospel, a most precious grace of the new covenant, and the everlasting glory of the Redeemer. A man may steal some gems from the crown of Jesus, and be guilty only of *petty larceny;* he may escape at last, like the cross thief—escape through the fire when his house is in a flame; but the man who would justify himself by his own works, steals the crown itself, puts it on his own head, and proclaims himself a king in Sion by his own conquests.

Since, therefore, faith is the *law* of the Gospel, the *term* of salvation, the *instrument* of obtaining every blessing, and the *general commandment* including all the rest, it must utterly exclude all justification by works. And the man who seeks to be justified by his passport of obedience, will find no passage through the city gates. He may talk of the tree of life, and soar up with his paper-kite to the gates of paradise, but will find no entrance. The gates belong to the Prince of Life, who is the real tree of life; and only they shall enter who own him for their liege-lord, and place their *whole* dependence on him, and seek a passage through his grace *entirely.* Such shall have a cheering taste of the tree below, and a joyous feast above.

You are peeping on my bag, doctor, for another fox, and here he is; a pretty brisk fellow, truly! How sharp he looks, and casts a gloating eye on you, as if he had a message for you; and now he opens.—"Doctor, I have listened to your talk, as I lay in the grazier's bag, and believe you are a greater fox than myself. Let the grazier look well to his purse, or he may find your fingers in it presently. I have many works to boast of; but you have none, it seems; and therefore raise a racket about faith. I must speak my mind freely, else my conscience will be loaded. All the honest foxes look upon you methodists as a set of crafty villains, and they would not trust a pullet's neck in any of your hands, notwithstanding all your sheepish looks. None can peep into a breast, you know; and there the instrument of faith is kept, which *hooketh* down salvation. But these *hooks*, instead of being gospel-hooks, may chance to prove fish-hooks; and I suppose you are angling for the grazier now, to catch him. The other night, as I was sauntering to a neighbor's henroost, I overheard some people talking of a slippery trick, lately played by a juggler. It seems he talked high of faith, and called himself a deep professor, and he proved much too deep for shallow people there. His nimble tongue first gained their admiration, then their confidence, and then their purses. He borrowed many pretty sums, and having fairly caught them with his fish-hook, he prudently retired. This may prove a caution to the grazier not to snap at your baited hook, but to rest upon his good works, as the foxes do." Why, doctor, this fox is quite a master of arts, and seems a notable advocate for good works. And I must confess some check seemeth wanting in the covenant of grace. Cheats will arise, and how must we deal with them, doctor?

Deal with them, sir! why, hang them, when detected, as Jesus hanged Judas. He had one religious cheat among his twelve, who made a penny of his master, but did not live to spend it. This Judas bids you guard against such cheats, but not be scandalized at the Gospel when they happen. You would not surely renounce honesty, because you have been cozened by a man who made a false pretence to it; nor would I renounce my creed because a sly professor proved a thief, and has been hanged.

But, sir, you quite mistake the matter, in supposing that the Gospel does not guard against licentiousness. A covenant of grace cannot allow of legal conditions, which may procure a *right* to life, in whole or in part; this would destroy the nature of the covenant. But it abounds with gospel checks, which answer the same purpose; and where they do not prove sufficient, nothing else would.

Naked faith, or a whole and simple trust in Jesus, is the gospel instrument which brings salvation. But though faith *alone*, apart from its fruit, is the saving instrument, yet it cannot be alone, or without its fruit, where it is saving faith, as St. James declares. And the Gospel, to prevent delusion, shews what is the fruit produced by faith. It bringeth heavenly peace, purifies the heart, and overcomes the world. Faith is genuine where these fruits are found. The believer is a real branch of the true vine, and receives his fruit from it. The fruit *shews* the branch to be alive, but does not *make* it so — it beareth fruit, because it is alive.

Where these fruits are neither found, nor truly sought, faith is not of God's operation; it is a dead, and not a living faith. It may be clear in Scripture doctrines, but has no real union with Christ, and of course no influence from him. It is not grafted in the vine, but tied to it with profession thread, and so is dead and withered. But, sir, the fruit of faith does not justify a sinner; and this must be oft repeated to check a legal heart, which is moved only by legal fears and hopes.

None feel the force of gospel motives, till they taste of gospel blessings. Hell and a gallows, proper checks in their place, keep some out of mischief, who find no comfort, nor expect it, in God's service; and a fond hope of making purchases in heaven puts some on almsgiving, and fasting, and prayer. Such only make account of obediience, as of a thing whereby they must be *saved;* and being told it cannot save them, because it is not *perfect,* they ask in much surprise, what then is it good for? Why, sir, it is *good* to glorify God for the mercy of a rich and free salvation — a grateful homage paid to a gracious God. And it is further *good* to evidence the truth of faith to ourselves and others.

When *joy and peace are found through believing,* and the sweet atonement is sealed on the conscience, a Christian crieth out, *I am* bought *with a price, and must glorify God with my body and my spirit, which are God's.* With Paul, he can say, *the love of Christ constrains me,* and feel its sweet compulsion. Gratitude begins to act, and love sharpens gratitude; and sights of glory, fetched in by faith, quicken both.

The legal hope of being saved by our doings is rooted deep in every human mind, and never can be rooted out, till grace has overcome it. It made a busy stir when the Gospel first appeared, and has raised ferments ever since. Very early, some cried out, *Except ye be circumcised, ye cannot be saved.* Had they suffered circumcision, as believing it a duty still required, and purposing by such obedience to *glorify* God; or had they used it, like Timothy, at Paul's instigation, for a more convenient spreading of the Gospel, no harm at all had been done. But when they seek to be *saved* by this doing, Paul takes fire, throws his hat up, and begins to exclaim, *Behold, I Paul, say unto you, that if ye be circumcised* (with this view), *Christ shall profit you* nothing. *For I testify* again *to every man, that is* (thus) *circumcised, he is a debtor to do the* whole *law. Christ is become of* no effect *to you, who are justified by the law: ye are fallen from grace.*

The Galatians did not seek to be *wholly* justified by works: no, they blended the two covenants together, as modern Christians do, and sought to be justified from both; partly from their own works, and partly from Christ. This appears from Paul's saying, *Christ is of* no effect *to you who are justified by the law: Christ shall profit you* nothing. Which implies, that the Galatians did expect *some effect* and *some profit* from Christ, as well as *some* from their works. Again, when Paul says, *Ye are debtors to do the* whole *law,* this also shews, they did not count themselves *such* debtors, but only sought a *partial* justification, by *sincere* obedience to the law.

The apostle's meaning in the fore-cited passage is plainly this: Whoever seeks to be justified in *any measure* by his works, such a one falls from grace, and becomes a debtor to do the *whole* law. Christ will justify you *wholly*, or *none* at all. Either take him as a *whole* Saviour, or he profits you *nothing*, is of *no effect* to you.

It matters not at all whether the work be ritual or moral that we seek to be *saved* by; whether it be parting with our cash in charity, or parting with our flesh in circumcision, which is the sorest work of the two. If we seek at all to be *saved* by any work of our own, *we fall from grace.* Therefore, when Paul had spoken first of circumcision in particular, he next affirms of the whole law in general, that *whosoever is justified by it is fallen from grace!*

Paul was eminent in ministerial labors and in Christian holiness; yet in the point of justification, *he counted all things but loss, in comparison of Christ.* His labors and his holiness, if rested on in any wise for justification, would have brought him loss instead of gain, and made Christ of *no effect* to him. He therefore desires to be *found in Jesus, not having his own righteousness* (to justify), *but that which is through the faith of Christ, the righteousness of God by faith.* In other words, he desires to be found at the bar of God, not in his own *personal* righteousness, but in the righteousness of his heavenly surety.

But you are waiting for more gospel-checks, I perceive, to prevent the abuse of faith. What think you, sir, of this? *Faith worketh by love.* It passed muster lately, yet wants to be reviewed; good troops are often exercised.

It is a two-edged sword, which sliceth off the wanton ears of an antinomian, and the saucy hopes of a legalist. Faith is here described as a *working* principle, a heavenly root producing heavenly fruit; and thus it slays Herodians and Sadducees. But though a working faith, it worketh not for hire like a laborer, but like a son for *love.* A child of God does not hope to purchase heaven by his works, but seeks with *loving* heart to glorify a heavenly father for the mercy of adoption ; and thus faith crucifies a Pharisee.

If you inquire of Habakkuk and Paul, who are lodged in the same apartment, both the Old and New Testament Saint will tell you, *The just shall live by faith.* Here they give you a believer's character, he is a *just* or righteous man ; and yet declare he does not *live* by his righteousness, does not gain a title unto *life* by it — he lives by *faith.* His new nature makes him hunger for *implanted* righteousness, as a *meetness* for heaven ; but his faith bids him seek an *imputed* righteousness as his *title* to heaven. He follows after righteousness as his proper business and delight; but sings at his work with Isaiah, *In the Lord shall all the seed of Israel be justified, and in the Lord shall glory.*

Again, you read, *Without holiness no man shall see the Lord.* A legalist would see the Lord *by* his holiness, by the merit of it, but he cannot; and an antinomian would see the Lord *without* holiness, but he must not. Thus a Christian man can neither see the Lord *without* holiness nor *by* it; which, though a truth, may seem a mystery to many.

Lastly. The Gospel declares roundly, that whosoever

liveth in the works of the flesh, in adultery, fornication, uncleanness, wantonness, idolatry, witchcraft, hatred, variance, emulation, wrath, strife, sedition, heresy, envyings, murders, drunkenness, revellings, and such like, shall *not inherit the kingdom of God.* For all who live and die in such works, plainly show themselves destitute of that faith which *purifies the heart, and works by love.*

And now, sir, I trust you will no more complain that faith is destitute of proper guards. No earthly monarch can be better guarded. If any more foxes are left in your bag, pray lug them out; I must be going presently.

Doctor, you shall have another quickly. I am dragging out his heels; and here he is. But how he grins at me! Sure, I do not half like his countenance. What is the matter, Reynard?

"Matter enough, master grazier! Why am I cooped in a bag, and bereft of liberty? I was born in a free country, and have a right to breathe free air. If I trick a lamb out of your fold sometimes, do not you trick a butcher too with worthless sheep? And does he not trick his customers with injured mutton? And do not they trick the butcher often out of his money? So your tricking, like the year, goes round; and the best of you is but a fox to his neighbor. When we borrow lambs or geese, necessity compels us. We must live by our wits, or not at all. You are satisfied we have no convenience for breeding lambs or poultry; and if we had, there is reason to suspect you would make as free with our folds and henroosts, as we do with yours. If harmless hares cannot well escape you, neither would our lambs and poultry. Besides, an honest fox, when taken in a henroost, no more complains of dying, than your good Christian folks complain of hanging, when taken in a burglary. But this we do complain of, as a very partial thing, that some of us, a little remnant, are picked out from the rest, and have wholesome food and lodging in a stable yard, while the rest are doomed to destruction. I am bagged for a hunt, and every day must live in fear of hounds; while the smirking fox, inhabiting a kennel, lives every day in peace and plenty like a gentleman. No reason can be given for this arbitrary choice, since all our natures are the same; and if bad, are but as we received them; nor can we make them better. We foxes often talk about morality, and like it fully as well as you; but we cannot live by honesty; it proves our utter ruin, and so we practise it as little as yourselves. Oh, master grazier, if you can reconcile this partial conduct towards foxes with common equity, never quarrel with your Bible-election. We have not wronged you, as you have wronged him that made you; and we may claim far better usage from you, than you can claim from your Maker."

Why, doctor, this fox preaches like a methodist; he must have been a curate at the tabernacle, or some recruiting sergeant to the countess; but he shall have to hunt to-morrow for his saucy sermon. I cannot bear the subject. Our vicar always shakes his head when he hears of election; and the schoolmaster makes a woful wry mouth at it. He will let his face down amazingly, when the word is only casually mentioned. Indeed my stomach rises sadly at the doctrine. It is a frightful notion, exceedingly discouraging, and seemeth not consistent with common equity. What think you of it, doctor?

Sir, I think the doctrine of election never can agree with human merit. One will be always barking at the other. Every man who seeks to justify himself by works, will loath the doctrine heartily, and load it lustily with most reproachful names. Yet men reject the doctrine, not for want of Scripture evidence, but for want of humbled hearts. We are not willing to be saved by *an election of grace* till we know ourselves, and find our just desert.

A furnace is the proper school to learn this doctrine in, and there I learnt it. Nor men nor books could teach it me; for I would neither hear nor read about it. A long and rancorous war I waged with it; and when my sword was broken, and both my arms were maimed, I yet maintained a sturdy fight, and was determined I would never yield; but a furnace quelled me. Large afflictions, largely wanted, gave me such experience of my evil heart, that I could look upon *electing grace* without abhorrence; and as I learned to *loath* myself, I learned to *prize* this grace. It seemed clear, if God had mercy for me, it only could be for this gracious reason, because *he would have mercy;* for every day and every hour, my desert was death.

Sir, the color rises in your face; and I shall take a hasty leave unless your staff is laid upon the floor. The fox, I find, must have a hunt to-morrow, for the hint he dropped-to-day; and the least I can expect is bastinading. I know the rancor of the human heart against this doctrine, for I have sorely felt it; and *charitably* thought that all its teachers were the devil's chaplains. Sir, I go directly, unless your staff is laid aside.

Here, take it, doctor, in your own hand, and then you

may be easy; but pray be very brief upon this matter, lest my choler should arise. I cannot stand a long fire upon election ground; and if your words are very rough, they may bring on a furious handy-cuff. For your own shoulder's sake, do not lay me on too thick and hard.

Plain speech, sir, is the best — such I give, and give without bitterness. If gall should mingle with my words, it will not drop from my lips, but trickle from your heart.

I ask then, are you not a sinner? And is not death the wages of sin? And very *just* wages, because appointed by a *just* God? As a sinner then, you deserve death; and every man that sins, deserves it also. And sinners, at the judgment-day, will be condemned, not because they were decreed to be damned, but because they did revolt from God, and break his righteous laws, and sought no hearty refuge in Christ Jesus. *The Son of man will gather out of his kingdom all them who* do iniquity, *and will cast them into a furnace of fire.*

No sinner then can urge a claim on God; for every one has forfeited his life. God, if he pleased, might reserve them all for destruction, as he did the fallen angels; or he may reserve some for punishment, by leaving them to follow their own wickedness; and be gracious unto others, by granting them repentance, faith, and holiness. And in shewing mercy unto these, he does no injury to others.

If you think that God may not withhold his mercy from some, while he sheweth it to others, or that he is *obliged* to shew it unto any, or to all, then he has no grace to give, but is a debtor unto man; and the covenant of grace is an empty name.

When traitors are condemned to die, it often happens that the king will spare some one at least, and hang the rest. And this act of *grace* may be shown to one or more, without a charge of *injustice* to them that are hanged. One has cause to bless his prince, while the others have no reason to complain.

And shall not the sovereign Lord of all be allowed to act in the same manner towards his *rebellious* subjects? Must his hands be tied up, that he cannot do what an earthly prince may justly do, shew mercy to some offenders without injuring the rest? This is hard indeed! But God will not be fettered by the cobweb cords which human pride has weaved for him. He will have grace to give, and justice to inflict: and will be glorified in both.

The provision of a Saviour gives no sinner right to *claim* the mercy of salvation. It only makes a way for God to exercise his mercy, in consistency with justice; but he may exercise it when and where he pleaseth.

The grace of God is called *free;* not because it is free for you or me or any one to *claim*, but free for God to *give* to whom he pleaseth. His grace is free, just as my alms are free: and grace is heavenly alms. Now my alms are free, because they are bestowed freely, where I like. If any could demand them justly, they would cease to be an alms, an act of grace, and prove a debt.

If men had due conceptions of the majesty and holiness of God, and of the traitorous nature, deep malignity, and heinous guilt of sin, their mouths would soon be stopped. But men forget their *real* state of condemnation, and dreaming of a claim on God through the fancied merit of obedience, grievously worm-eaten, they quarrel with the doctrine of election. And indeed the doctrine cannot harmonize with any human claim arising from a pure covenant of works, or from the mongrel covenant of faith and works, transported from Galatia into Britain, and carried by her convicts to the colonies. No; the doctrine of election is altogether built upon a *pure* covenant of grace, and shakes a friendly hand with this. Here God may grant, or may withhold his mercy, as he pleaseth; since all are in a state of condemnation, and none can justly say unto him, *What doest thou?* This, sir, may suffice to vindicate God's *justice* in electing grace; and his justice is well grounded upon equity. He needs no court of chancery.

Neither has this doctrine any *real* tendency to discourage sinners, when they truly seek salvation through Jesus Christ. It is not expected that any one should know himself a *chosen vessel*, before he seeks salvation. This must be known by seeking. He cannot peep into the rolls of heaven, to see if his own name be written there, nor needeth such a peep. His business lieth with the *written* word on earth, which tallies with the rolls in heaven. *Secret things belong to God; but what is revealed belongs to us, and to our children for ever.*

Now, in the written word, a *decree* of God is found, which shews who are the chosen and the saved people — *He that believeth, and is baptized, shall be saved.* The chosen people, therefore, are a race of true believers, convinced by God's Spirit of their ruined state; endowed with divine faith, by which they seek to Christ for help; and seeking do obtain pardon, peace, and holiness. And an experience of these blessings brings assurance of election. Thus the *written* word unfolds the secret rolls of heaven.

By grace a sinner is enabled to believe ; and through believing finds salvation, witnessed to his heart by the Holy Spirit.

Jesus Christ, the *bread of life,* is freely offered in the Gospel to every hungry famished soul. Such are prepared for the bread, and the bread prepared for such. And these should never pore upon the doctrine of election, but muse upon the Gospel promises, and call on Jesus confidently to fulfil them. He turns no real beggar from his gate however degraded. His heart is lined with sweet compassion, and his hands are stored with gifts. He has supplies for all wants: legs for a lame beggar, eyes for a blind one, cordials for a faint one, garments for a naked one, a fountain for a filthy one, and a rope for a sham beggar, who asks for mercy, and yet talks of merit.

Every one who feels the plague of his heart may come to Jesus. He gives them all a gracious invitation, and will afford a hearty welcome. Hear his words—"*Him that cometh unto me I will in no wise cast out*"—*in no wise!* though vile as Manasseh, debased as Magdalen, guilty as the cross-thief, or ten times more so, Jesus will *in no wise* cast him out. Strange tidings to a Pharisee!

But a weary soul who is *sick, and poor, and blind, and miserable and naked,* should come just as he is—just as the patients in Judea did, and not stay to fit himself for a cure. This is a sorry trick of the legal heart, which wants to *purchase* favor, and take the work out of the Saviour's hands. The feeling of our sickness makes us *fit* for the physician ; and when we seek to him, every fancied recommendation of our own must be cast aside, like the robe of Bartimeus, else it twines about the feet, throws a sinner down, and prevents his walk to Jesus.

It is the Saviour's office, as it is his honor, and his heart's delight to save a sinner freely; to call, and wash, and heal, and clothe, and feed a prodigal at his own expense. He asks no recommendation but his misery and helplessness, and does relieve his patients now, as he relieved them in Judea, out of mere compassion. All that seek in his appointed way will be saved graciously, and love the Saviour heartily. He makes them happy, wise, and holy, and they give him all the praise. He puts the crown at last upon their head, and they return it to his feet, as a due acknowledgment that the crown was purchased by his merit, and bestowed through his mercy. Thus Jesus will be ever glorious, ever lovely in a ransomed sinner's eyes; and eternity will seem too short to utter half his praise.

Now, sir, what discouragement can you find in this doctrine to make it frightful? The Gospel bids us *give all diligence to make our calling and election sure.* Such as feel their ruined state are graciously invited to partake of mercy; and all who seek with diligence are assured they shall find; and when they find the peace and *love of God shed in their hearts by the Holy Ghost,* an inward evidence of their election is obtained, and by a growth in grace it is confirmed.

Thus an awakened sinner who feels his misery has no cause to be alarmed at the doctrine; and a sinner fast asleep will commonly despise it. He wants no drawings of God's Spirit; he is *wise* enough to draw himself; nor needs a shepherd's care to fetch him to the fold; he is *strong* enough to fetch himself; nor can bear the Lord should say, *I have chosen you;* he is *old* enough to choose for himself. He can *climb* into the fold by his own nimble legs, and keep himself there by his ready wit—no thanks to the shepherd. And he looks and talks so bravely, one is almost grieved to hear the shepherd say *a climber is a thief;* and by that word condemn him to the gallows.

Sinners perish through security, and this doctrine of election brings a little friendly thunder to arouse them. They think salvation is the work of man, and presume they may repent and turn to God just when they please—to-morrow or the next day, as well as in the present day, and so are unconcerned about it. But here they find an awful truth, *It is not of him that willeth, nor of him that runneth, but of God that sheweth mercy.* It is therefore time to look about them, to *ask, and seek, and knock, lest the door should be shut.*

But what avails our seeking, you reply, unless we are elected? Sir, I say again, your business does not lie with the *secret rolls* of heaven, but with the *written word* on earth; and the written word declares, *Ye shall seek and find me when ye shall search for me with all your heart.* Whoever thinks himself an elected person, and does not seek, as God requires, with all his heart, will find himself most dreadfully confounded. And such as seek with all their heart, yet doubt of their election, will find at length that God is their covenant-God in Christ. And when by seeking they have found him so, they will some time be made to see that grace alone, electing grace, did give them both the *will* to seek and the *power* to find.

None can come to Jesus, *except the Father draws them.* Yet sinners do not perish, because they *cannot* come, but because they *will not* come. Jesus says — "*Ye* will not *come to me that ye may have life.*" Man's ruin lieth wholly in his own *perverse will.* He cannot come, because he will not. Help enough is provided were he willing: but he will not heartily accept of Jesus as his only Prophet, Priest, and King; his heart will not submit to be *wholly* saved by grace through faith.

When the will is well subdued, and grace alone subdues it, Christ is ready for a sinner, and the promises invite him sweetly unto Christ — *Whosoever will, let him come;* and again, *Ho, every one that thirsteth, come.*

Thus salvation is of the Lord *alone*, and damnation *wholly* from ourselves. Men perish because they *will not* come to Jesus; yet if they have a will to come, it is *God who works the will in them;* grace, electing grace, both draws the will, and keeps it steady; and to grace be all the praise. Well, sir, any more chattering foxes in your bag?

Yes, doctor, one more; but the last served me such a scurvy trick, I have no heart to drag this other out. It may answer fully as well to borrow Reynard's face, and play the fox myself.

Your doctrine of election, I confess, is bravely sweetened by another portion of your creed, called perseverance. If the former seems a sour pill, this is quite a honeycomb. I never heard till lately of this doctrine, and learnt it then by accident. Last midsummer I went to Gamble fair, and when the market was well over, a knot of graziers, old acquaintances, dined with me at a public house. Being seated round a table, a pert young fellow stepped into the room, who swung his hat into the window, and thrust a chair among us, to partake of the ordinary. His name, we learned afterwards, was Mr. *Fulsome;* and his mother's maiden name was Miss *Wanton.* Mr. *Fulsome* was mighty still at dinner, and played his knife and fork exceedingly well; no man better. But when the cloth was removed, and some few tankards had gone round, Mr. *Fulsome's* face looked like the red lion, painted on my landlord's sign, and his mouth began to open. He talked swimmingly about religion, and vapored much in praise of perseverance. Each fresh tankard threw a fresh light on his subject, and drew out a fresh head of discourse. "No sin, he said, can hurt me. I have had a call, and my election is safe. Satan may *seize* me, if he please; but Jesus must *replevy* me. What care I for drunkenness, or cheating, or a little lying? These sins may hurt another, but they cannot hurt me. Let me wander where I will from God, Jesus Christ must fetch me back again. I may *fall* a thousand times, but I shall *rise* again. Yes, I may fall exceeding *foully.*"——And so he did, doctor; for instantly he pitched with his head upon the floor, and the tankard in his hand. The tankard was recovered; but no one thought it worth their while to lift up Mr. *Fulsome;* nor did he rise from his foul fall, according to his prophecy. We left him silent on the floor when the shot was paid. Oh, doctor, what must we say of such professors?

The very same, sir, that Paul says, *Their damnation is just.* Such scandalous professors are found at all times in our day, and Paul's day; yet he will not renounce the doctrine of perseverance; but having given these licentious men their dose, he declares a firm persuasion afterwards, that *nothing shall be able to separate* true believers *from the love of God, which is in Christ Jesus.*

Jesus Christ, the shepherd of the flock, declares, *I give unto my sheep eternal life, and they shall never perish, neither shall any pluck them out of my hand.* Yes, he affirms, *The mountains shall depart, and the hills be removed, but my kindness shall not depart from thee, neither shall the covenant of my peace be removed, saith the Lord, who hath mercy upon thee.*

What right have you to pray for perseverance, unless it is a gift of the covenant? You may pray only for what is freely promised; and what is promised has been purchased for believers; and being purchased for them, will be surely given to them, else the purchase were in vain.

Pardon of sin is promised — *I will forgive their iniquities, and remember their sins* no more; therefore I may ask for pardon.

Grace is promised to subdue our evil nature, *Sin shall not have dominion over you; he will subdue our iniquities;* therefore I may ask for sanctifying grace.

Perseverance too is promised — *I will make an* everlasting *covenant with them, that I will* not turn *away from them to do them good; but I will put my fear in their hearts, that they shall* not depart *from me;* therefore I may ask for persevering grace, and should ask with confidence, as David did. *The Lord,* he says, *will perfect that which does concern me;* therefore he prays, *forsake not the works of thine own hands.*

God's promises are the foundation for our prayers; and

were designed, not to make the means of grace needless, but to stir men up to a diligent use of them. A gracious heart maketh this use; but a corrupt heart turns the grace of God into wantonness, and no legal terrors would prevent it. The thunders, lightnings, earthquakes, which shook Mount Sinai, almost terrified the Israelites to death; yet a day after, we find them brisk and jolly, setting up an idol, and dancing round it merrily. And such is human nature, almost killed with fear at an awful providence, yet laughing at that fear when the shock is over. Nothing but the grace of God can set the heart right, and keep it steady.

The doctrine of perseverance affords a stable prop to upright minds, yet lends no wanton cloak to corrupt hearts. It brings a cordial to revive the faint, and keeps a guard to check the froward. The *guard* attending on this doctrine is sergeant *If;* low in stature, but lofty in significance — a very valiant guard, though a monosyllable. Kind notice has been taken of the sergeant by Jesus Christ and his apostles; and much respect is due unto him from all the Lord's recruiting officers, and every soldier in his army.

Pray, listen to the sergeant's speech! If *ye continue in my word, then are ye my disciples indeed.* If *ye do these things, ye shall never fall.* If *what ye have heard, shall abide in you, ye shall continue in the Son and in the Father. We are made partakers of Christ,* if *we hold steadfast unto the end. Whoso looketh and continueth* (that is, *if* he that looketh does continue) *in the perfect law of liberty, that man shall be blessed in his deed.*

Yet, take notice, sir, that sergeant *If* is not of Jewish,

but of Christian parentage ; not sprung from Levi, though a son of Abraham ; no sentinel of Moses, but a watchman for the camp of Jesus. He wears no dripping beard, like the circumcised race ; and is no legal blustering *condition* to purchase man's salvation, but a modest gospel *evidence* to prove the truth of grace. He tells no idle tales, that the sheep of Christ may perish, and a child of God mistake his way, while his guide is fast asleep, and ramble down to hell ; but knowing there are various works which are but mimics of a work of grace, he kindly standeth on the king's highway of faith, producing peace and holiness ; and telleth passengers, *if* you contiuue walking in this way, your perseverance proves your faith is true ; for faith, which comes from God, endures, and brings men safe to God.

Perseverance *makes* us not in Christ, but *shews* we are so ; unites no branch unto the vine, but proves it is united ; merits not the crown of heaven, but shews our walk is heavenward. A persevering walk is an *evidence* that we are blessed with persevering grace ; and *are not of them who draw back unto destruction, but of them who believe to the saving of the soul.*

When this little sergeant is neglected, and appeareth to be scouted, bad effects ensue. Chaffy hearers, resting on a shallow work, are dancing after all new doctrines, and stirring up confusion. Upright people often grow remiss, and through a sauntering foot are apt to trip, and lose their evidences : preaching, too, becomes a sore travail, a needful rod for the preacher's back, to make him friendly with the sergeant ; and occasion may be taken, by them who seek occasion, to revile the doctrine.

When Jesus says, *I give unto my sheep eternal life, and they shall never perish*, this secures the perseverance of the saints. And when he further says, *If ye continue in my word, then are ye my disciples indeed*, this shews that actual perseverance in the way of faith and holiness must be my *evidence* to prove that I am one of his sheep. A *belief* of the doctrine of perseverance cannot save me, without the *grace* of perseverance.

In the Old Testament, the saint's perseverance is thus expressed, *They that are planted in the house of the Lord shall flourish in the courts of our God ; they shall still bring forth fruit in old age ; they shall be fat and flourishing ; to shew that the Lord is* upright — that is, faithful to his word, and does not forsake his people.

In the New Testament, perseverance is described by the *good ground which hears the word, and* keeps it, *and brings forth fruit with* patience.

This doctrine yields no real shelter to licentiousness or laziness. If perseverance is promised to the saints, then I must be found persevering in the path of duty and the means of grace, else the doctrine does condemn me, and destroy my evidence.

St. Peter exhorts all Christians *to make their calling and election sure ;* not taking up this matter on light grounds, but using all diligence to be *assured* of it, *by adding unto faith, courage, knowledge, temperance, patience, godliness, brotherly kindness, and charity.* His meaning is, prove your grace by a growth in grace ; where heavenly seed is sown, it brings a harvest. And there is need of such an exhortation. Appearances of grace and faith are often found, which flash and sparkle for a while, like meteors in the sky, and then vanish quite away.

Some, like the foolish virgins, bear a lighted lamp, and keep up Christian fellowship, yet have no oil in their vessels, no grace in their hearts: some, like Judas, preach the gospel-word, and cast out devils from the hearts of others, but remain themselves the devil's bond-slaves: some, like stony ground, receive the word with eagerness, and find refreshment from it; yet having no root, they take offence at persecution, and take their leave of Jesus: to some God gives *another* heart, as he gave to Saul, but not a *new* heart; and such may prophesy, as Saul did, for a season; and taste the joy, which prophets taste, yet be rejected from the kingdom, as Saul was. The sower's parable instructs us, that many are awakened, enlightened, and reformed in a measure, who seem hopeful for a time, yet having not a rooted faith in Christ, they dwindle quite away. These are awful evidences of that solemn and repeated word, *Many are called, but few are chosen.*

No dependence can be placed upon a present reformation, nor on short-lived impressions from the word of joy or sorrow; but a *growth in grace, and in the knowledge of Christ Jesus*, must be sought, as the crowning evidence of all the rest. The vineyard which the Lord planteth *will be kept and watered by him every moment; kept* by him, that none may hurt it; *watered* by him, that it may thrive and bear fruit. The thriving and fruit-bearing of a vine discovers it to be of God's planting.

But you ask, are none recovered after sad and heinous

backsliding? Yes, sir; but not without the grace afforded of a bitter sad repentance. When backsliders live and die in a course of sin, without repentance, they are lost undoubtedly. This case is determined in both the Testaments. Jesus says, *Except ye repent, ye shall all perish.* And Ezekiel saith, *When a righteous man turneth away from his righteousness, and committeth iniquities, and dieth in them, for his iniquity that he hath done, he shall die.* Such final backsliding is the case of all the stony and the thorny ground hearers, and shews the heart was never truly brought to God. Men may seem to be religious, walk in *righteous* paths for a season, and be called *righteous* men, to difference them from the openly profane, and yet be unconverted men. By a sober education they may walk a while decently, as Jehoash did, though not devoutly; be civilized, though not evangelized; or they might hear the word from a Samuel's mouth, as Saul heard, and become *another* man, as Saul became, but not a *new* man. If backsliders had been real children, God would have scourged them well with scorpions, and broken all their bones, as David's were, and fetched them home with streaming eyes and bleeding heart.

When repentance is afforded after heinous backsliding, a few examples are recorded in the Scripture, to encourage such to call on God, and hope for mercy. And when Jesus breaks a heart for sin, his blood will heal it. But if backsliders fancy they must all be restored by repentance because David was restored, and Peter was, they might as well suppose they must all be translated into heaven without dying, because Enoch and Elijah were.

To sin, presuming on repentance and a future call, is such a devilish motive, and carries such a cloven foot, as shews a case bad indeed. This was not Peter's case, nor David's. The most alarming thunder in the book of God is levelled at such horrible presumption. *If any bless himself in his heart, saying, I shall have peace though I walk after the imaginations of my heart, to add drunkenness to thirst,* (that is, sin to sin,) *the Lord will not spare* that man; *but the anger of the Lord and his jealousy shall smoke against* that man; *and all the curses which are written in this book shall lie upon him.*

Indeed, doctor, I can see no reason to object against the doctrine of perseverance, when attended by the sergeant's guard. While they walk hand in hand together, the doctrine is a spur to diligence, and the sergeant is a check to wantonness or laziness. But how comes it that the world takes such high offence at these doctrines, and loathes the preachers and professors of them? Nay, we are told that some very honest folks, who are cast in a gospel-foundry, often ring a fire-bell to quench these very doctrines. And you may think it makes us titter when we hear a cry of fire, and see some engines from the foundry playing on the tabernacle-pulpit. It is pretty sport for us, when the gospel-men pull noses, and the gospel-dames pull caps. Such frays make us laugh delightfully, and yield a venison feast for the squire and the vicar. "Now these rogues begin to quarrel, we shall hear of all their tricks," they cry. When the dean of Tottenham died, his chapels, we supposed, would tumble down of course; but they keep upon their legs, we hear;

and the pulpits are becrowded most amazingly. Our schoolmaster is reputed a very topping scholar. He can write Italian hand, read a Latin dictionary, manage vulgar fractions, and give you twenty nimble reasons for every thing; and he says, the doctrines of grace will never be abandoned by those who are tinctured with them. For every one who slips into them drops into a quagmire, and is swallowed up directly. He compares the doctrine to Polyphemus's den, where many went in, but none came out; all were eaten up alive in the cave by the monster.

Sir, I perceive your schoolmaster is an arch fellow; and, like his neighbors, useth wanton tricks to put modest truth out of countenance. A fool's cap thrust upon the head of a serious truth, or a grave judge, will make them both appear ridiculous, when nothing else could. However, truth will not be thrust out of doors, though often put to the blush. She may change her countenance, but cannot change her nature, nor will desert her post. Yet, if religious truth meets with lewd opposers, I must confess she sometimes meets with wanton advocates, who hang upon her skirts, and claim acquaintance with her, and bring disgrace upon her, though she disclaims them utterly.

Scandalous professors are found in every age, who warp the doctrine of grace to sanctify their wickedness. Like the spider or the toad, everything such lewd men feed upon is turned into poison. Paul speaks of these, and says, *Their belly is their God, and they glory in their shame.* Peter calls them *Spots in their love-feasts; sporting themselves with their own deceivings; cursed children; having eyes full of adultery, and hearts exercised with covetous practices.* And Jude can scarcely keep his temper while he brands them as *brute beasts; filthy dreamers, walking after their own lusts: raging waves of the sea foaming out their own shame; clouds without water, carried about with every wind; wandering stars, for whom is reserved the blackness of darkness for ever.*

Such professors will arise at all times, and give a just offence to serious minds; and because these *brute beasts* are always babbling about faith and grace, this sets the world of course against the doctrines. They are condemned as poisonous, because abused by hypocrites, and every preacher of the doctrines is supposed to be an open or a secret advocate for vice. Even Satan seems a much more harmless creature than a Calvinist. If he has one cloven foot, a Calvinist, be sure, has two.

But, sir, the abuse of doctrines is no argument to prove the doctrines themselves are hurtful. The blessings of providence are fully as much abused as the doctrines of grace, yet none reject the providential blessings, because of their abuse. If all my countrymen were drunkards and gluttons, this would be no argument for my rejecting food and drink, but a good caution to use them temperately. And if my brethren, who profess the doctrines of grace, should all agree to wear them as a cloak for wickedness, this would be no reason for my rejecting the doctrines, but a strong caution not to wear the cloak myself. The Apostles did not reject the doctrines of grace, because a wicked use was made of them; no more should you or I.

The common run of Christians do not regard the doctrines of grace, yet thousands live in open sin, and cheer their hearts in sin, by saying God is merciful. The doctrines of grace cannot be more abused than the mercy of

God is, nor afford a sweeter handle for licentiousness; yet no horrid outcries are raised at this abuse. Many mind it not, and others pass it softly over with saying it is wrong. But sure God's honor is as much concerned in this abuse as in the other. And since men can bear to have the mercy of God abused, but take a violent offence when the doctrines of grace are perverted, this sheweth that the mere abuse of these doctrines is not the *chief* ground of the world's outcry. The doctrines themselves are hateful, because they batter human pride, undermine all human merit, lay the human worm in the dust, and give the glory of salvation wholly unto God. Nature cannot bear this, she would not have salvation as a *lost*, but as a *decent* sinner; nor become an heir of glory by a mere election of God and faith in Jesus, but by some noble plea of merit; nor would she walk in duty's path through the Holy Spirit's aid, but by her own gouty ankles. With some reluctance she endureth to go halves with Jesus, but will never bear to be wholly saved by grace. It is so pitiful a way — so much beneath her dignity! What? If she is become a captive, and the devil's captive, she was once an empress, and will never wear a crown through another's generous purchase, but by her own exploits, and decent share of merit.

It is not possible to preach the doctrines of grace, nor even to profess them, without the world's indignation and censure. If every preacher was a Timothy, and all professors were Nathanaels, still the world would hold them in abhorrence, think them Satan's troops, and call them wolves in sheep's clothing. Paul affirms that himself and his fellow-laborers were slandered as licentious men, who said, *Let us do evil, that good may come.* And Peter intimates that all the Christians were *spoken against as evil-doers.* Now, sir, if the preachers in the purest age of the church were slandered as licentious men, and professors were reviled as a race of evil-doers, it is no marvel that the slander rolls along through all succeeding ages.

And what could give occasion to this slander? Not the evil conduct of the first preachers and professors, but their nauseated doctrines, which made old nature sick. Preachers said, and converts did profess, that *men are justified by faith, without the deeds of the law; chosen of God before the foundation of the world; called by grace; kept by the power of God, through faith unto salvation;* and *saved not according to their own works, but according to God's purpose and grace.*

Such preaching, though attended with much practical instruction, appeared so licentious, that a heathen stomach revolted at it. Loose as the Gentiles were, they could loathe a Christian for his supposed evil principles; and did condemn them all, apostles and their flocks, as the *filth of the world, and the offscouring of all things.*

And if this was the case in the purest age, what else can be expected in succeeding ages? But you say, we sojourn in a baptized country. True; the country swarmeth with baptized rakes, baptized worldlings, and baptized infidels. A watery profession, without the Spirit's baptism, will never wash the heart from pride, and subdue it to the Gospel doctrines; and legal righteousness will set the heart still more against them. *No one can truly bear the doctrines till he cannot bear himself.*

Jesus Christ inviteth them that are weary of themselves,

and laden with their guilt and sinful nature. Only such receive him in Judæa, and only such receive him in Great Britain. These are prepared for his Gospel, know what poverty of spirit means, and feel that brokenness of heart. which God delighteth in, and where he only dwells.

These are the Gospel subjects; but alas! how few. And where must we find them, in leather or prunello, in camblet or in sarsenet? They are a *little flock* indeed, who have been taught to say with Job, and say with deep compunction, *We abhor ourselves.* Yet Job was called a *perfect* man, by one who knew what is in man; but Job wanted breaking down, before he could truly say, *Behold I am vile.* And when the furnace had well melted him, disclosed his dross and filthy scum, and made him *loathsome* to himself, then the work was done. The furnace cooled presently, his sorrows fled away, and peace and plenty smiled on him.

The doctrines of grace are utterly repugnant to the pride of our Arminian nature; yet none forsake the doctrines who have gained a clear sight of them. They are abused by some, as every good thing is, but are abandoned by none. Arminians, who have received a ray of gospel-light, desert their ranks frequently; but a Calvinist will never leave his standard; he dies at the foot of his colors. A clear sight of grace is so exceeding glorious, it keeps the heart steady to the doctrines.

Perhaps you think a Calvinist maintains his ground, because it is bestrewed with roses, and suits licentious purposes. But, sir, this calumny is grown exceeding stale. It was broached first in Paul's day, and poured on him liberally, and sprinkled on his hearers; and has begrimed his followers in all succeeding ages. If the slander sticks on us, it cleaves to Paul abundantly; because he tapped this nauseous vessel which turns the human stomach, and makes it rave with indignation.

These doctrines suit a contrite spirit; and are drank, not as a Circe's bowl, to intoxicate the mind, but as a grace-cup to cheer the heart, and keep it steady under trials. They do not prove a *monster's den*, as you suppose, where all are eaten up who enter in; but a *banquet-house*, where pilgrims find such sweet repast, they have no will to leave it.

If I seem tedious on this article, the misguided zeal of some, I hope, well-minded people, has constrained me; who have taken most outrageous pains to blacken Calvinism. Whatever ridicule a sparkling fancy could suggest, whatever filth or ordure could be raked together, has been cast upon it. The looseness of a few is charged on all the rest; and a devil's coat is put upon a Calvinist, like some condemned heretic; and in this flaming raiment he is held aloft, as a horrid bugbear, to frighten simple-hearted people.

Well, but doctor, one thing somewhat gravels me, that these doctrines will not relish with the present age, though they are established. The law, the homilies, the articles, the prayer-book, all afford protection to them, and yet they cannot stand upon their legs. Pray, what makes them prove so rickety?

Sir, your question may be answered by another. Can any good thing keep its head above water in the present age? If the doctrines of grace are rejected, is not the word of God despised too, and the house of God deserted, and the name of God blasphemed everywhere? The Bible, like an old almanac, is either cast out of doors, or cast upon a solitary shelf, to be buried there in dust, and covered with a winding-sheet weaved by a spider. How should the doctrines keep upon their legs when the Bible, which contains them, is fallen upon the ground?

Unless a *spirit of grace* is poured out upon a land, the *doctrines of grace* cannot be heartily received, because they fight with every dictate of depraved nature. The first lesson to be learned in Christ's school is, *deny thyself*, every thing that belongs to *self*, not *self*-pleasing only, and *self*-interest, but all *self*-sufficiency, self-will, self-potence, and self-righteousness; and these are heavy crosses to be taken up.

The law was *established* with divine solemnity among the Israelites; yet they were evermore deserting this establishment, and warping to idolatry. And how were they reclaimed? By a prophet's mouth, you say. True; but a prophet's mere preaching could no more reclaim the people, than a prophet's dancing. God gave a promise to his prophet, *I will pour upon the inhabitants of Jerusalem the* Spirit of grace *and supplication*, and so the work was done. Where the *Spirit of grace* fell, a change was wrought.

Even so it fares with the Gospel, which can no more be kept on foot, than the law was without a supernatural power. Men will desert the doctrines and the precepts of the Gospel, for these go hand in hand; nor can human establishments prevent it. Establishments may keep up forms, but Christ alone can give the power. A fanciful alliance may be framed between church and state; but the church's whole support is from the church's Head. *The government is laid upon his shoulders ;* and he will never prosper doctrines which oppose his grace. Such preaching will be chaff and stubble, and the preachers grow contemptible.

When a Christian church becomes exceedingly depraved ; when *its nobles are as ravening wolves ; and its prophets daub them with untempered mortar ; when its watchman are grown blind, love to slumber, and are looking every one for his gain ; and the people, great and small, given unto covetousness*—then, unless *the Lord revives his work by pouring out his Spirit from on high*, the church's candlestick is quite removed, and she becomes a sister to the African and Asiatic churches.

Mahometanism is the gulf provided by the Lord, for his abandoned churches to be drowned in. They first deny the God who made and bought them, which drives them to the synagogue of Arius ; another gentle step leads them to the chapel of Socinus ; and half a pace more brings them briskly to the mosque of Mahomet.

Doctor, I am told by the vicar that his brethren drop the doctrine of justification by faith *alone*, because it seems unfriendly to morality. And he says the *Whole Duty of Man* was sent abroad, as a public bellman, to cry the doctrine down. The clergy now are straining all their nerves in support of common duties, and seem so fervent in this matter, that a jackdaw dares not perch upon the steeple while they are shouting in the pulpit for morality. They give the lash sometimes when the squire keeps from church, but do exclaim against all thieving and hedge-breaking most delightfully. Indeed, their lungs have been so often strained by uncommon zeal for morality, that they are forced to wind up matters very speedily. Many cannot roar above ten minutes at a preaching for want of breath; and others are constrained to keep a journeyman to shout for them.

Sir, morality, like beauty, is a charming object, but, like beauty, often is made up with paint. Such seems morality at present; a pretty plaything when dandled on a consecrated cushion, or chanted in a modern midnight conversation, but will not keep men from an alehouse. The people, who are chiefly loaded with morality are the booksellers; and they have got a shopfull, but are rather sick of the commodity, and long to part with it. Though gilt and lettered on the back, it moulds upon a shelf, like any Bible; and Mr. Hales' tract on salivation will post away through ten editions before a modest essay on morality can creep through one.

The *Whole Duty of Man* was sent abroad with a good intent, but has failed of its purpose, as all such teaching ever will. Morality has not thriven since its publication, and never can thrive, unless grounded *wholly* upon grace. The heathens for want of this foundation could do nothing. They spoke some noble truths, but spoke to men with withered limbs and loathing appetites. They were like way-posts, which shew a road, but cannot help a cripple forward; and many of them preached much brisker morals than are often taught by their modern friends. In their way they were skilful fishermen, but fished without the gospel-bait, and could catch no fry. And after they had toiled long in vain, we take up their angle-rods and dream of more success, though not possessed of half their skill.

God has shown how little human wit and strength can do to compass reformation. Reason has explored the moral path, planted it with roses, and fenced it round with motives, but all in vain. Nature still recoils; no motives drawn from Plato's works, nor yet from Jesus' gospel, will of *themselves* suffice : no cords will bind the heart to God and duty but the cord of grace.

Man is conceived and born in sin ; what can he do? Nature is sunk and fallen ; and nature's creed is this, Video meliora proboque, deteriora sequor—I see and I approve the better path, but take the worse. Nature may be *overruled* for a time by some violent restraints; but nature must be *changed*, or nothing yet is done. The tree must first be made good before the fruit is good. A filthy current may be stopped ; but the brook is filthy still, though it cease to flow. The course of nature may be checked by some human dam, yet opposition makes the current rise, and it will either burst the dam, or break out other ways. Restrained sensuality often takes a miser's cap, or struts in pharisaic pride. Nothing but the salt of grace can heal the swampy ground of nature, as Elisha's salt, a type of grace, healed the naughty waters and the barren grounds of Jericho.

The law is not given to make a sinner *righteous*. Through the *weakness of his flesh*, it has no power to justify or sanctify him. It shews the path of duty, but neither lends a crutch to lame travellers, nor gives a heavenly title unto sinners. Paul knew the use of the law, and declares, *It was added because of transgressions*. It was *added* to the promise made to Abraham, which contained the covenant of grace ; and was added *because of transgressions,* that men might know what heinous things they were.

Again, *The law entered, that the offence might abound.* The offence (τὸ παράπτωμα, the fall) of Adam, was a sin with penalty of death; but no such penalty had been annexed to any sin beside *murder*' from Adam unto Moses. Men knew themselves to be offenders, but did not know that death was the penalty of each offence, till the law pronounced *a curse on every one who continued not in all things.* Then they saw that death was the wages of every sin. Thus when the law entered, the offence, with penalty of death, did abound; and the law entered, that such offence *might* abound, to certify sinners of their *lost* condition, and their utter need of a Saviour. Hence we read, *The law worketh wrath,* not our justification, but our condemnation; and *by the law is the knowledge of sin.* The law, by its penalty, discovers my *condemned state;* and by its spirituality, discloses my *corrupted heart.* Therefore, Paul says, I, *through the law, am dead to the law* — dead to all expectations of relief from it, either to justify my person, or to sanctify my nature. And his conclusion is this — *Wherefore the law is our schoolmaster, to bring us unto Christ, that we might be justified by faith.* The law sends us unto Jesus, not with recommendations in our hand, but with condemnations in our bosom; and is meant to empty us of every fancied legal hope arising from our own obedience, and force the heart to seek salvation *wholly* by grace, through faith.

When the law has done this office, and sent a sinner, wounded, poor, and naked, to the good Samaritan, then it becomes a *rule of life* in the Mediator's hand. And Jesus, having justified a sinner by his blood and righteousness, sanctifies him by his Word and Spirit. The work belongs to Christ *alone*, as Saviour ; and a believer's business is to live upon him wholly, calling on him fervently, trusting in him stedfastly, and, by a life of faith, to receive from his fulness a supply for every want. No real holiness of heart, nor true morality in life, can be had but through him, and by faith in him. He is the true vine, producing every branch, with all its leaves and grapes ; and is the *green fir-tree, from whom our fruit is found.*

For a century past, the noble building of God's grace has been propped up with legal buttresses. Moses is called in hastily to underprop his master Jesus. *Galatian* anvils are bought up, and gospel-doctrines hammered thin, and beaten out upon them. Jesus can behold no cast of grace in his own gospel; and Paul, were he alive, would cry aloud, *Who has bewitched you, O foolish* Britons ?

Now, sir, I ask, what good effects have been produced by this modern gospel ? A century is time sufficient to give us full experience of it. Do we find more praying families, more crowded churches, and more empty jails ? Are ropes pulled oftener in a chiming steeple, and stretched seldomer at Tyburn ? Can we travel roads with more safety, and sleep with fewer bolts upon our doors ? Are play-houses and gaming-houses become exceeding rare ; and their owners grown very meagre, quite abashed at their occupation ? Have we more preaching bishops and pains-taking clergy, more staunch patriots and upright lawyers, more gentle masters and faithful servants, and more fair dealing practised in buying and selling ?

Alas, sir, you know, and I know the contrary. Gluttony and drunkenness, cursing and swearing, gaming and gambling, diversion and dissipation, are become so common, as to make the fashion : and nameless sins, the last scum of a filthy land, are bubbling in the pot apace, and boiling over. Wickedness wears no mask and fears no censure. Ever since the new gospel shewed its face, profaneness and infidelity have been pouring in, like a sweeping rain, and overflowed the land. God has lost his worship, Christ has lost his office, Scripture has lost its credit, and morality has lost its carcass. It has become a pageant, held up in a pulpit, but seldom noticed out of it; and as for holiness, it is the land's abhorrence. The Christian title, *saint*, not applied in Scripture to apostles, but to all believing churches, is become a name exceedingly fulsome. A Christian nose will wind up like a bottle-screw at the mention of it; and Esau cannot vent his spleen on Jacob more effectually than to cry, "you saint."

Sir, these things are notorious, and a judicial consequence of departing from the Scripture doctrines. God will bear no witness to any doctrines but his own. All endeavors for a reformation will be blasted, when they build on human merit, will, and power, and are not grounded *wholly* on the grace of Christ. A legion of discourses have been published on morality, and a little host of volumes have appeared against infidelity; yet immorality and infidelity are making rapid progress through the land. And how can this be well accounted for, if the modern gospel is the gospel of Christ Jesus?

Where the doctrines of grace are truly preached, a spirit of grace will be poured forth to make the word effectual. For thus the Lord speaketh, *As the rain cometh down from heaven, and watereth the earth, and maketh it bring forth and bud, so shall* my word be ; *it shall not return unto me void, but shall prosper.* And again, *If the prophets had caused my people to hear* MY WORDS, (had truly delivered my doctrine) *then they should have turned the people from their evil way, and from the evil of their doings.* And this was spoken also of such prophets *as ran before they were sent,* had no commission from the Lord. Yet of these the Lord says, *If they had caused the people to hear* my words *they should have turned them from their evil ways.* Though they were interlopers, or even hypocrites, yet, like Elijah's raven, they should have carried meat in their mouth to feed another, which they tasted not themselves. Judas, though himself a devil, casteth devils out of others, when he went in Christ's name, and preached Christ's word.

Now, sir, the case standeth thus :—God has promised a reformation when his word is truly preached ; but no reformation is produced by the modern preaching. Things are visibly declining from bad to worse. Therefore we must conclude, either the word of a faithful God is fallen to the ground, or his word has not been preached faithfully. If God is not in blame, the preachers are and must be so.

For a long season the good old church doctrines have been much forsaken ; by some they are derided, and by many are deserted. Yet no doctrines can build the Church of Christ up but those which planted it. We may labor much in lopping off loose branches of immorality and infidelity, yet nothing will be done effectually till the axe is laid to the tree's root. The root is cankered, and while it remains so, the lopping off a cankered branch will only cause more cankered shoots.

The fall of Adam, and the total ruin of man's nature by that fall, together with his *whole* recovery by Christ, and through faith in him, are become exploded or neglected doctrines. Yet these doctrines are the ground-work of our religion, and prove the need of *regeneration* as well as outward *reformation ;* shew the want of a *new nature* as well as *new conduct.* Scripture represents mankind as dead in sin, and dead to God ; and dead souls can have no power to help themselves. *We are without strength,* and therefore God has laid help on one that is *mighty,* able to save unto the uttermost.

Men are rightly treated in a reading-desk, and called by their proper name of *miserable sinners ;* but in a pulpit they are complimented on the dignity of their earthly, sensual, devilish nature ; are flattered with a princely will and power to save themselves ; and ornamented with a lusty badge of merit. Justification by faith, the jewel of the gospel-covenant, the ground-work of the reformation, the glory of the British church, is now derided as a poor old beggarly element, which may suit a negro or a convict, but will not serve a lofty scribe, nor a licentious gentleman. And the covenant of grace, though executed *legally* by Jesus, purchased by his life and death, wrote and sealed with his blood, is deemed of no value till ratified by Moses. Paul declares, *No other foundation can one lay,* beside *that which is laid, Christ Jesus.* But men are growing *wise above what is written,* and will have two foundations for their hope—their own fancied merit added to the meritorious life and death of Christ.

If an angel should visit earth, and vend such kind of gospel as is often hawked from the press and pulpit, though he preached morality with most seraphic fervency, and till his wings dropped off, he would never turn one soul to God, nor produce a single grain of true morality, arising from the love of God, and aiming *only* at his glory.

When Nicodemus waits on Jesus, he receives instruction, such as every hearer should receive from his teacher. The sermon is recorded as a model for the ministers of Christ to copy after. Nicodemus appears to be a very upright man, though somewhat timid; he was a teacher too in Israel, διδάσκαλος; and of course explained the two tables, and preached what we call morality. He also was a lowly man, and therefore wanted more instruction, and he came to Jesus with a high opinion of his character, believing him to be a *prophet, a teacher come from God.*

Had Nicodemus lived in the present age, he would have been esteemed a topping gospel minister, and might have made a notable archdeacon. For, though a stranger to the *new birth*, and to *faith* in Christ's *atonement*, he was a teacher of morality, a moral man himself, and had full faith in Jesus as a *prophet.* Well, he comes to Christ, and expects, no doubt, a famous lecture on morality, and perhaps some handsome compliment for himself; but, lo! he is told, *Except he is born again, he cannot enter into the kingdom of God*—his kingdom of grace and glory. A moral conduct shall avail him nothing, without a new birth, a new nature from above. The Jewish ruler was a stranger to this doctrine as some modern teachers are, and asks a mighty staring question about it; and seemed much bewildered, even after Jesus had explained the doctrine.

Yet Nicodemus, as a teacher in Israel, must have read his Bible, and of course understood the necessity of *reformation*, or a *new moral conduct.* And who can be a stranger to this matter, Heathen, Jew, or Christian, whose conscience is not wholly seared? But if Jesus meant a reformation of life by regeneration, his behavior to the ruler was very disingenuous, and cannot well be justified. For on this supposition, Jesus only proposed a matter to Nicodemus, which he knew perfectly well; but proposed it craftily under a new name, or a metaphorical expression, which he knew not, and then takes occasion to upbraid the ruler with his ignorance, *Art thou a master in Israel, and knowest not these things?* Jesus therefore must either meant something more than mere reformation of life, or his conduct towards Nicodemus will appear crafty and captious.

If by regeneration Jesus did not intend a *moral reformation* of life, but a *spiritual renovation* of nature, a real but secret work of the Holy Spirit on the souls of men, producing a new and spiritual service, and divine communion in that service, then his reproof of the ruler was just, because he might have learned the doctrine of regeneration from Ezekiel, where God says, *I will take away the heart of stone and give you a new heart and a new spirit; and I will put my Spirit within you.* Herein consists God's work of *regeneration;* and the *true reform-*

ation results from it, yet by the Lord's hand, for so it follows, and *I will cause you to walk in my statutes, and keep my judgments, and do them.*

So, when Moses gives his dying charge to Israel, he tells them, *The Lord thy God will* circumcise *thy heart, and the heart of thy seed, to love the Lord thy God with all thy heart and with all thy soul.*

Jeremiah also preaches the same doctrine, *I will give them one heart and one way; and I will put my fear in their hearts that they shall not depart from me.*

When Jesus had declared to Nicodemus the necessity of *regeneration*, he then speaks of the *atonement*, and of *justification by faith; as Moses lifted up the serpent in the wilderness, even so must the son of man be* lifted up; *that whosoever* believeth *on him should not perish, but have eternal life.* And so the conference ends.

The Spirit's birth brings a *meetness* for heaven. It teaches men to offer spiritual sacrifices; but it gives no right to pardon, nor any claim to eternal life. These blessings are wholly treasured up in Christ, and are obtained *only* through faith in him; even as you heard just now, *Whoso believeth on him hath eternal life.* Therefore Jesus conducts the ruler through regeneration to the atonement and justification by faith, and there ends — ends with what truly finishes the Christian character, a *whole* dependence upon Jesus Christ, even after spiritual life is received, and manifested by a holy walk.

When the doctrines of regeneration and justification by faith become despised or deserted doctrines, the labors of the clergy will prove useless, their persons will grow cheap, their office seem contemptible, and they at length may be ashamed of their *function* and their *livery.*

The present age would fain be called a learned age, and the giddy people think themselves a wise people — *wise to do evil, but to do good have no knowledge.* Reason flirts at revelation, merit spurns the thought of grace, tapers would outblaze the sun, and human fancies far outweigh the truth of God. But, sir, I must be moving.

A word or two more, doctor, and then we take a friendly leave. Your visit to the grazier will certainly get wind. Every creature will be staring as you walk through the parish. Your look and gait are very primitive; and your beaver would fill a bushel. A dozen skimming-dish hats, such as the gentry wear, might be scooped from it. To-morrow I expect the vicar at my house, to dine upon a good fat capon, and he will surely make inquiries after you. Can you put a brief account of faith into my mouth, which may lie at my tongue's end, ready for him when he comes? He will hear what is said patiently; and if he does not approve, he will not revile. He rails at nobody, and has never had a single squabble with the parish since he came, about his tithe eggs, pigs, or turnips.

Faith in Christ, sir, implies not only a *hearty belief* of the Saviour's doctrines, but a *whole dependence* on the Saviour's person, as our prophet, priest, and king. It requires a careful use of the means of grace, but forbids all trusting in the means. I must read the word of God with care, yet not rely upon my own ability to make me wise unto salvation, but *wholly* trust in Jesus, as my prophet to open my dark understanding, and direct me by his Spirit into all saving truth. I must watch against sin, and pray against it too; yet not rely upon my own strength to conquer it, but *wholly* trust in Jesus as my king, to subdue my will, my tempers, and affections, by his Spirit; to write his holy law upon my heart, and influence my conduct to his glory. I must be zealous of good works — as zealous to perform them, as if my pardon and a crown of glory could be purchased by them; yet *wholly* trust in Jesus, as my priest, to wash my guilty conscience in his purple fountain, and clothe my naked soul in his glorious righteousness, thereby receiving all my pardon and my title to eternal life.

The life of faith is thus expressed by Paul, *Run with patience the race set before you, looking unto Jesus* — looking unto him with a single eye continually; and looking so by prayer and faith, as to receive supplies for every want.

Faith is the master key to the treasury of Jesus; it opens all the doors, and brings out every store. A heart, well nurtured in this precious grace, finds the gospel rest. In time of danger, sickness, or temptation it flutters not, nor struggles hard to help itself, but *standeth still and sees the Lord's salvation.* The eye is singly fixed on Jesus, the heart is calmly waiting for him, and Jesus brings relief. Faith calls, and Jesus answers, "Here I am to save thee."

Indeed, doctor, I am quite charmed with this account of faith; it is just what our church homilies tell us. It secures the interests of holiness, obedience, and good works, and gives the whole glory unto God. Why, this is right; man is saved, and God glorified; man is brought to heaven through grace, and sings eternal hallelujahs for it. I wish we heard a little more about this gospel-faith, and indeed a little more about Bible-sin and holiness ; but these names, I think, are growing out of date. Doctor, I have no wine to offer ; but you shall take a glass of my Holland gin, before you go ; it is right special. The weather is hazy, and may require it ; and my heart is quite free to give it.

Sir, I thank you, but I drink no drams. They are too violent and forcing for a Christian, whose understanding should be free and calm. Indeed, no sort of cordial now is wanted : I am enough refreshed if you are satisfied.

Farewell, doctor.

Farewell, sir ; grace and peace be with you.

THE END.

www.ingramcontent.com/pod-product-compliance
Lightning Source LLC
LaVergne TN
LVHW011212110826
845150LV00006B/1413

* 9 7 8 1 4 2 5 5 1 7 5 4 0 *